D1265949

DISCOVERY & EXPLORATION

Exploring the Polar Regions

HARRY S. ANDERSON

JOHN S. BOWMAN and MAURICE ISSERMAN
General Editors

®
Facts On File, Inc.

Exploring the Polar Regions

Facts On File, Inc.
132 West 31st Street
New York NY 10001

Library of Congress Cataloging-in-Publication Data

Anderson, Harry S.
    Exploring the polar regions / Harry S. Anderson.
       p. cm. —(Discovery and exploration)
       Summary: Begins with the three expeditions of John Franklin, England's most honored and respected Arctic explorer, and covers exploration and discovery of the Arctic and Antarctic regions through the present. Includes bibliographical references (p.).
    ISBN 0-8160-5259-X
       1. Polar regions—Discovery and exploration—Juvenile literature. [1. Polar regions—Discovery and exploration.] I. Facts On File, Inc. II. Title. III. Series.
    G587.A54 2004
    910'.911—dc22   2003023034

Facts On File books are available at special discounts when purchased in bulk quantities for businesses, associations, institutions, or sales promotions. Please call our Special Sales Department in New York at (212) 967-8800 or (800) 322-8755.

You can find Facts On File on the World Wide Web at
http://www.factsonfile.com

Text design by Erika K. Arroyo
Cover design by Kelly Parr
Maps by Dale Williams and Patricia Meschino

Printed in the United States of America

VB FOF 10 9 8 7 6 5 4 3 2 1

This book is printed on acid-free paper.

This book is dedicated to my wife, Michela,
and to
Eric, Alexander, and Michael.

NOTE ON PHOTOS

Many of the illustrations and photographs used in this book are old, historical images. The quality of the prints is not always up to current standards, as in some cases the originals are from old or poor quality negatives or are damaged. The content of the illustrations, however, made their inclusion important despite problems in reproduction.

CONTENTS

PREFACE

All exploration, involving by definition the unknown, has within it elements of danger. But the story of polar exploration is special. The story of polar exploration, from the 1600s to the present, is not just of voyages into the far north and the far south. Nor is it just about the new lands and seas and islands discovered or the failures and deaths and vanished expeditions. The real story is that of men of a certain cast of mind who willingly pitted their will and their determination against an environment as hostile as any to be found on Earth. There are no regions as hostile to human life as the Arctic and the Antarctic, and there were no expeditions to the polar regions that did not have inherent in them the distinct (and likely) possibility of death and disaster. That possibility underlies many of the events in this volume.

Generations of mariners came back from the frigid zones with frozen noses, amputated fingers and toes, their health permanently damaged by bouts of scurvy and months or years of inadequate diet. Yet incredibly, there was no shortage of new recruits to replace the unfit. Seamen signed on for voyages that might last for years; they parted from their loved ones with no guarantee that they would ever return. And for the ordinary able-bodied seaman, the financial rewards were small.

Because of the terrible hardship of polar exploration, the objectives of the early expeditions (before the 20th century) changed somewhere between the home port and the first encountered frozen strait. Or perhaps the objective, the purpose of the mission, changed when the captain and the navigator realized that the charts available were wrong and the maps insufficient to reveal where the ship was or which was the best way to go.

Whenever it occurred, at some early point the objective became that of survival. Frozen in solid ice, somewhere (but not sure exactly) west of Greenland, waiting out the winter, waiting for a summer thaw that did not come that year, the early Arctic explorers aboard their imprisoned ship must soon have turned their attention to the diminishing food and fuel supplies and the dozens of men sick with scurvy. The explorers of the 17th, 18th, and 19th centuries soon learned that all of their efforts must be directed to just reaching the general area of intended exploration and getting out alive. And so the early story of polar exploration tends to be the story of men and ships not reaching their destinations yet managing to survive and return home with the purposes of the mission unfulfilled.

The failure was not that of the leaders nor of the brave crewmen; the failure was that in the early period of such endeavors, the expeditions were wholly unprepared for the conditions that they were required to meet and overcome. It is amazing that exploration, in the 18th century, for instance, was as successful as it proved to be. Certainly the accomplishments of the expeditions of that period were due to the heroic efforts of the commanders and captains who persevered and succeeded, using ships and equipment wholly inadequate for the job. The history of polar exploration is filled with the names of commanders of expeditions whose courage and determination sustained the spirits and lives of the party and brought ships and crews back to safety against all odds.

Vilhjalmur Stefansson, himself a pioneering Arctic explorer, in his book *The Friendly Arctic* (1921), speaks of a period of exploration that he calls the "Romantic period." In this phase of polar activity, leaders such as Sir John Franklin, Roald Amundsen, Robert Scott, and Sir Ernest Shackleton (to name but a few) were men of great strength, whose vision and determination brought about the achievements of their missions. In his book, Stefansson also points out that this kind of leadership so essential at that time was no longer so important in the 20th century; instead, modern exploration was more about teamwork, organization, and technology.

Some recent historians have been critical of the great early pioneers of polar exploration. Franklin, for example, has been charged with negligence in the preparations for his final expedition, Scott has been accused of bringing about his own disaster for similar reasons, and Robert Peary's conquest of the North Pole will always be under a cloud of suspicion. Such criticism does not seem to take into account the conditions under which these men had to carry out the aims of their missions. It is the responsibility of a fair-minded account of polar exploration to evaluate leadership performance always in the context of the times and circumstances. This volume has undertaken just such an accounting.

Another interesting aspect of polar exploration is that it can be examined as a developing function of technological change. There is no point in observing that Franklin's fate would have been different if he had had a radio, that Scott would not have died if an airplane could have dropped supplies, or that Robert Peary would not have lost eight toes if he had had a nuclear submarine. The fact is that the story of early polar exploration is about *not* having convenient life-saving items. As technological innovations are introduced (and perfected), gradually one sees the ease and success rate of polar missions increase. As ships are better built and strengthened, fewer expeditions are caught and crushed in the ice. As the steam engine replaces sail power, the range and power and versatility of the ships increased greatly. Every new development—the wireless radio, the airplane, nuclear power, navigational systems— brings about immediate change in the mode and degree of efficiency of polar exploration.

One of the elements that makes the study of the earliest as well as more recent polar exploration interesting and fruitful is the abundance of records and accounts written by the explorers themselves. Since much of the exploration was carried out by ship, there are logs and journals of the voyages, often recounting the events of every single day of the expedition. Such journals are often detailed in navigational and operational business, but many are expanded with personal observations about the strange and new vistas encountered, the unexpected brutal weather, and the morale and condition of the crew members. Some of the leaders of Arctic expeditions took an interest in the customs of the Inuit and wrote insightful things about those hardy, courageous people. Often the writing of the explorer becomes philosophical: Bravery, despair, and the cruel aspects of nature are subjects that come to the mind of the explorer in the desolation of the polar wastelands. And so there is a wealth of information that comes from the impressions and thoughts of the explorers themselves.

There are a great number of autobiographical accounts that are rich in details of the facts and the context of exploration. Franklin recounted the hardship and the horror of his first Arctic expedition in *Narrative of a Journey to the Shores of the Polar Sea* (1823). Amundsen described the first transit of the Northwest Passage in *The North-West Passage* (1908) and his being the first to reach the South Pole in *The South Pole* (1912). Isaac Hayes revealed the observations and experiences that led to his faulty assumptions about the Arctic Ocean in *The Open Polar Sea* (1867). No better account has ever been given about the unimaginable conditions of the Antarctic winter than Richard Byrd's *Alone* (1938) in which he tells of his experience of living in solitude, buried under the ice for protection from the cold in Antarctica. Sir Robert McClure, William Parry, George Washington DeLong, Elisha Kent Kane, Scott, Shackleton, Peary, and Fridtjof Nansen: These are but a few of the many explorers who gave a full, illuminating account of their exploits. So the story of polar exploration is made vivid and compelling by the firsthand reports of those who engaged in it. And because so many people were intent on reading the firsthand accounts of expeditions, the books—even those published in the 19th century—are still to be found on many library shelves.

Because polar exploration (and exploration in general) has always had a strong appeal to a wide audience, there is also an abundance of writing *about* polar explorers and expeditions. A number of explorers themselves have written not only about their own exploits but about the voyages of others and about the north and south regions in general. William Scoresby's *Account of the Arctic Regions* (1820), Nansen's *In Northern Mists: Arctic Exploration in Early Times* (1911), and Stefansson's *Three Voyages of Martin Frobisher* (1938) are three good examples of this kind of account. Many scientists and would-be explorers in earlier days wrote about the expeditions that were occurring in their time. Alexander Dalrymple, for example, authored *Voyages and Discoveries in the South Pacific Ocean* (1771). John Barrow, secretary of the Admiralty during Franklin's time, shares his misconceptions about the Arctic as well as his passionate belief in and support of the search for the Northwest Passage in *A Chronological History of Voyages into Arctic Regions* (1818). In this study, Barrow tries to put the search for the Northwest Passage into a historical framework, to include the exploration activity of his own time and under his own leadership.

In more recent times, a great deal has been written by scholars and scientists about all aspects—historical and present day—of polar exploration and scientific discovery. The selected reading list in the Further Information section at the end of this volume, though but a fraction of the material available, reflects the range and extent of 20th-century scholarship and suggests the continuing popularity of this field of study. The establishment of many polar research centers outside the regions, and the presence of many polar studies programs (particularly of "Arctic studies") in North American universities is further evidence of the interest in, and the importance of, continued study in the developments that have followed exploration.

The popular fascination with polar exploration—as evidenced to this day by the many books and films about Shackleton's epic trip, for example—has been responsible for a secondary product of exploration: fiction about exploration and explorers, related voyages, and all manner of adventures in the polar regions. The first writing to blend the facts of exploration and the interplay of characters in the Arctic region is in the medieval Icelandic sagas, the exciting accounts of the earliest Norwegian excursions to (and settlement of) Greenland, Iceland, and North America. (One of the finest available translations, by Magnus Magnusson, is identified in the reading list.) More contemporary works include novels about the Arctic and the Antarctic by James Fenimore Cooper (*The Sea Lions*), Jules Verne (*An Antarctic Mystery*), and James M. Houston (*The Ice Master,* a novel about 19th-century whaling). Recent writers of note are Canadians Pierre Berton and Farley Mowat, who have woven their experiences in the far north into novels that accurately illuminate the regions and the people who inhabit them.

How the explorer reacted to the circumstances encountered is often best expressed in the words of the participants themselves, so whenever possible quotations from the logs and journals of the expedition are cited to enhance the despair (and often beauty) of the moment. No armchair reader can fully experience the terror of an Antarctic blizzard or understand the desperation of eating a leather boot (or the flesh of a faithful sledge dog) or visualize the beauty and threat of an iceberg, but the words of the explorers, these expressions of innermost feelings, reveal the inner life of exploration.

The essays or discussions in the sidebars throw light on a variety of topics: the physical elements encountered by the explorers, the provisions and gear used by explorers, the peoples and animals encountered, lesser-known explorers and expeditions, and background to put major developments into perspective. All these support, amplify, and embellish the main narrative.

Of special appeal to those interested in the polar regions are the various films—both documentary and fictional—available on VHS or DVD, a sampling of which are contained in the Further Information section at the end. Still more information can be obtained through the various Web sites that focus on the two polar regions as well as some of the key explorers active in those regions.

In that spirit of objectivity, this study has attempted to present, as clearly as possible, the conditions under which polar exploration was carried out and the conduct of both leaders and men within those very confining conditions. As an example, the story of exploration begins with maps, and this volume provides maps of all the relevant locales and features. But the reader must have a sense of the geographic features of the regions involved, for a map can show only where point A and point B are, but not how to get from A to B if the intervening passage is frozen. Therefore, the text and maps in this volume work together to provide a full sense of the conditions confronted by the explorers.

The photographs and illustrations also serve to make the conditions of early exploration more vivid to a contemporary reader. Like a map, a picture is incapable of creating the stark reality of the polar regions, in all their beauty and fearsomeness. But a picture can go a long way toward suggesting the underlying hardship and travail that are the very heart of polar exploration. And often a photograph can reveal the satisfaction of achievement for the explorer who met and conquered all obstacles.

There is still much exploration to do in the Arctic and the southern continent. There are islands in the Canadian Archipelago seen and charted but never set foot on. Such unvisited places exist because there are more important things to do, not because they are, in the old sense, inaccessible. Eventually, they too will be like the North Pole, where aboard the *Yamal*, a Russian icebreaker, a tourist can drink champagne and if daring enough, plunge into the icy water for a quick swim at the top of the world. And there are many regions in Antarctica, photographed by airplanes, but still untrod by explorers. Yet for many years now, tour groups have been sailing to Antarctica and stepping ashore to observe and photograph the penguins or seals.

But the story of polar exploration does not end with tourists frolicking at the North Pole or expensive holidays in Antarctica. The significant consequence of the opening of the polar regions is the establishment of the multitudes of research stations that produce observations, measurements, and data crucial to all areas of scientific inquiry. And remarkably, the work at both poles is done in a spirit of international cooperation. This is the best possible result of exploration.

New findings and discoveries constantly proceed from ongoing scientific work. It is true that most of the polar landmasses have by now been discovered and explored, but this should not lead the present and future generations to think that the subject is now "wrapped up." As this book will make clear, there are many number of issues that remain controversial or at least require and repay further investigation. For example, the question of Scott's responsibility for the tragic end of his expedition to the South Pole continues to arouse debate, and as recently as 2001, Susan Solomon, a meteorologist with the National Oceanic and Atmospheric Administration, argued in her book *The Coldest March,* that it was the unpredictable abnormal weather that defeated his expedition, not poor planning. Not all students of this episode accept this theory. Another mystery that continues to be debated is why Franklin and members of his expedition began to die while they still had plenty of food and before the effects of the extreme climate took their toll. After all, other expeditions survived longer periods while trapped in the same Arctic ice. Various investigators argue that the Franklin expedition's deaths were caused by some combination of botulism and lead poisoning from the cans of food they were eating. This theory is most thoroughly laid out by Scott Cookman in his book *Ice Blink.* Again, this is not accepted by all who study this episode, reinforcing the point that polar exploration and polar studies still provide challenges.

Finally, it is the historical background of exploration of the regions that still has the power to fascinate. Exploration becomes more than going somewhere and finding something; it becomes the story of human aspiration, of strength and weakness, and of perseverance and undaunted determination. Perhaps the fascination comes from observing human activity at its outer limit of potential and capability. In the case of polar exploration, its story from 1555 to the present may well represent the last age of heroism.

1

AN EXPEDITION VANISHES

In February 1845, the British Admiralty appointed 59-year-old Sir John Franklin to lead a mission intended to discover and navigate the final unknown parts of the long-sought Northwest Passage, a waterway through North America leading to the Pacific Ocean and the riches of China and the Orient. Fifty-nine was an advanced age for such an assignment, given the proven rigors of Arctic exploration. But Franklin was eager to go; solving the puzzle of the Northwest Passage would be the crowning achievement of his distinguished career. Franklin had certainly shown, by his three earlier Arctic expeditions and his years of subsequent public service, that he was a man of great fortitude, unyielding commitment to duty, and clearsighted judgment.

Franklin's first expedition to Arctic Canada (his very first voyage to the Arctic had not proceeded beyond Greenland) had taken place in 1819–22. After a number of false starts, Franklin made his way from Fort Enterprise on Canada's Great Slave Lake to the Coppermine River; from there he canoed to the mouth of that river, on the Coronation Gulf. Traveling east along Canada's northernmost shore line,

he carefully explored and mapped 300 miles of coast line to the edge of the Kent Peninsula, where he named the farthest point he reached

At the age of 59, Sir John Franklin headed an unsuccessful search for the Northwest Passage after having led three other Arctic expeditions. *(Library of Congress, Prints and Photographs Division [LC-USZ62-103581])*

Point Turnagain. The return to Fort Enterprise, in the dead of winter, was one of the most horrific ordeals ever endured by Arctic explorers. Nine of the 21 expedition members died on that journey. Although the expedition had managed to map several hundred miles of uncharted territory, it had failed in its primary mission. Even so, Franklin returned to great acclaim in London as the man who had survived, as he recorded in his journal, by living on stew "made from moss and leather boots."

In 1825–27, Franklin undertook his second expedition to North America, this time to continue his mapping of the western part of the Northwest Passage. Franklin, more experienced, completed this mission without any loss of life. Furthermore, he managed to chart another 600 miles of coastline, and his partner, Dr. John Richardson, mapped an additional 1,000 miles. After his return to England in 1827, Franklin was generally regarded as the greatest living English explorer.

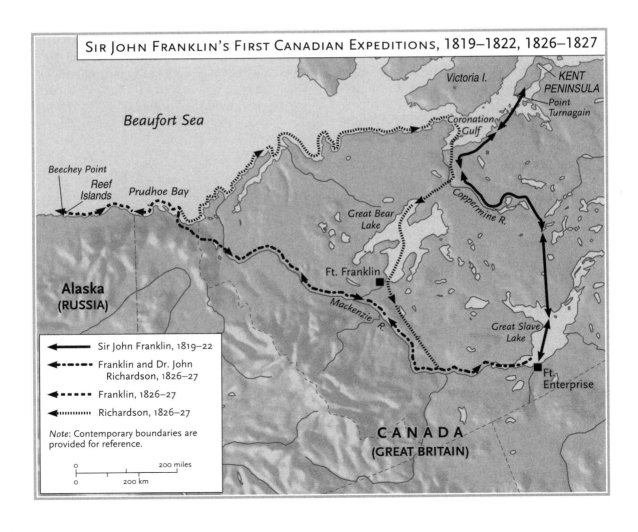

SIR JOHN FRANKLIN'S FIRST CANADIAN EXPEDITIONS, 1819–1822, 1826–1827

Officers and Gentlemen

Sir John Franklin was in command of the 1845 expedition to discover the last remaining portion of the Northwest Passage. Directly under him were the captains of the two expedition ships, the HMS *Terror* and the HMS *Erebus*. The two captains, Francis Rawdon Moira Crozier and James Fitzjames, present an interesting contrast that provides some insight into the workings of the Royal Navy.

Crozier, captain of the *Terror,* was, at the time of Franklin's selection, the most suitable explorer in England for the mission. He had spent 35 years in the Royal Navy, many of them with the best of the British commanders, including the experienced Arctic mariners William Parry and James Clark Ross. Crozier had spent 10 years in the ice, at the North and South Poles. He had been on five Arctic missions, and he had already served on the *Erebus* as well as the *Terror*. He had far more experience than Franklin, and he was younger, more up to date, and more dynamic. But Crozier was Irish, Presbyterian, and not a gentleman — at least not by the English standards of the time.

Captain James Fitzjames, on the other hand, had no Arctic experience. At 33, he was quite young but most promising and was rising fast into the top echelon of Royal Navy officers. Fitzjames came from a wealthy, aristocratic family; he was well educated, socially graceful, and at the time known as the "handsomest man in the navy." He was also a hero and had performed a number of self-sacrificing, perilous actions to justify that term. Finally, Fitzjames was a specialist in the use of the steam engine.

It is probable that John Barrow, secretary of the Admiralty, who chose the officers, thought that the strength of these two men would augment and complement the abilities of Franklin. Although it appears that Crozier proved to be the hardier of the two, in the end none of the qualifications of Crozier or Fitzjames — or for that matter, Franklin — counted when confronting the Arctic challenge.

THE PERFECTLY PLANNED EXPEDITION

So it was that the expedition of 1845 under the great John Franklin was expected to be completed with relative ease. Speaking with the optimism and confidence felt by the lords commissioners of the Admiralty, their secretary, Sir John Barrow, said, "There can be no objection with regard to any apprehension of the loss of ships or men."

Never before had an expedition been so carefully prepared. The two vessels for the mission, HMS *Erebus* and HMS *Terror,* were both tried and true veterans of polar exploration. The *Erebus,* the flagship of Franklin's expedition, was captained by the young star of the Royal Navy James Fitzjames. The *Terror,* captained by Francis Crozier, was the sister ship of the *Erebus.* In preparation for this voyage, both ships had undergone modifications to make absolutely sure they could withstand the terrible force of the arctic winter. The sides were strengthened by additional layers of oak planking up to eight feet thick in the bow portion. The bow was then covered with thick plates of sheet iron, to crush the ice that would lie in the way of passage. Massive timbers inside the hull crossed from beam to beam to strengthen the sides and prevent crushing by pounding ice floes. More powerful steam engines—locomotive engines, weighing 15 tons—and propellers were installed so that progress was not solely dependent on the power of the wind. Even the rigging was changed to make it more manageable by fewer crewmen.

The interiors of the *Erebus* and the *Terror* had also been refurnished with new cabins and bunk spaces for officers and men. There was adequate space available in the holds of the ships for extra fuel and the mountains of provisions that could last for three years, even though Franklin expected to be back in England within a year. London's most prestigious grocers, Fortnum and Mason, had supplied the expedition with more than 65,000 pounds of meat pickled in salt in barrels; as a safeguard, more than 40,000 pounds of meat and vegetables preserved in tins were also packed aboard. Another hefty item was the 10,000 pounds of lemon juice for the prevention of scurvy, a disease caused by a lack of Vitamin C. Sugar, spirits, raisins, tea, concentrated soup, dried peas, and 100 pounds of mustard were only some of the other foodstuffs loaded aboard in great quantity. Of course the seaman's staple, hard tack—a hard baked biscuit of flour and water—was in great abundance; 68 tons of flour were included in order to make more biscuit when it was needed.

The two ships were lavishly equipped in other ways. There were libraries with almost 3,000 books on every subject. There were musical instruments and costumes for the dramatic performances that would entertain the men and while away the long arctic nights. A variety of scientific instruments were available to officers and men to carry out observations and conduct experiments. Many of the crew, particularly officers, took along articles for their personal comfort and pleasure: fine silver settings for formal dinners, evening formal dress, and extra sets of shiny leather dress boots. Some officers brought such items as writing desks, walking sticks, and favorite foods.

THE FRANKLIN EXPEDITION SETS FORTH

Thus it was that in spring 1845 the mission of the great Sir John Franklin was awaited by all with every expectation of success. As the *Times* of London stated in May of that year, "The expedition may be attended with great results." On May 19, 1845, the *Erebus* and the *Terror* weighed anchor and sailed down the Thames from London. The expedition proceeded to Disko harbor, Greenland, to load final supplies and to rendezvous with the supply ship *Baretto, Junior.* There, at Disko, the sheep, pigs, and cattle brought over by the *Baretto, Junior* were slaughtered and loaded aboard the *Erebus* and the *Terror,* providing the expedition with fresh meat for the initial stages of the voyage. Final letters to friends and family were entrusted to the master of the *Baretto, Junior* to take back to England.

Franklin's orders from the Admiralty were both vague and direct. He was to proceed north in Baffin Bay and turn west into Lancaster Sound, which was known to be the eastern starting point of the Northwest Passage. He was then to sail west as far as a point up to then known simply as Cape Walker. Not far beyond this cape, William

Parry had noted that further passage was blocked by ice, so Franklin was instructed to follow any likely waterway to the south, to the mainland of Canada. Failing this route, he was to try to the north. Most of all, he must always bear west, until he reached the Bering Strait (which would be the end of the Northwest Passage.) The orders really were saying "find the Northwest Passage and navigate it." What the orders did not take into account was that the whereabouts of Franklin, should the mission find itself in trouble, could only be guessed.

On July 28, 1845, the *Erebus* and the *Terror* were in Baffin Bay anchored to an iceberg, waiting for favorable weather to enter Lancaster Sound. Some of the Franklin expedition officers were that evening entertained by a Captain Dannett on his whaler, the *Prince of Wales*. Dannett reported in his log that the explorers were all well, "in remarkable spirits, expecting to finish the operation in good time." The next day the *Erebus* and *Terror* moved off into the mist and must have very soon encountered conditions that began to affect the "remarkable spirits" of the voyagers.

The party reached Cape Walker, which they found to be the headland of a very small dot of land, Russell Island. Even though it was still summer, there was ice everywhere, barring passage to the west (Barrow Strait) and to the south. Franklin, following one of the options of the orders, headed north via the Wellington Channel, hoping that he could bypass the frozen section of Lancaster Sound (which became Barrow Strait at its western end). Rarely does the Arctic traveler escape ice by going north; somehow, however, Franklin forced his way up the Wellington Channel and back down the western side of Cornwallis Island, fighting through icy waters the entire way. He found himself back where he had started, in Lancaster Sound, with passage to the south and west still blocked. Franklin retreated to tiny Beechey Island, just off the southwest corner of massive Devon Island.

There, for the first time, on this windswept barren island, the explorers must have had a hint of what lay ahead, even though they had their comforts and entertainment. Food was still plentiful; although the fresh meat was long gone, there were thousands of pounds of salted beef and pork; there were canned vegetables and pickles; hot soups, raisins, sugar, chocolate, and the daily ration of strong, sweet rum, swigged down with hot water. In the evenings there were dramatic productions—musicals—and the men delighted in seeing their officers, dressed as fancy females, hamming it up in romantic comedies. The more serious minded had the well-stacked library to read in. Although the cold outside was terrible, the ships were warm: islands of light and heat in the frozen desert.

THINGS BEGIN TO GO BAD

In the middle of the first winter on Beechey Island, an unexpected and terrible sickness spread through the entire expedition. The first man to die was John Torrington, on January 1, 1846; two days later a second crewman died. Others were ill but recovered; in early April a third man died. It was suspected that the cause was the canned "preserved" food—whether the meat, vegetables, or soup. Tin can after tin can (12 pounds each) was opened, and some appeared to be satisfactory while others contained a soupy, putrid mush. What they did not know, though, is that at least some of the contents were apparently poisoned. Not all who have investigated the fate of these men agree on the cause, but it appears that the contents of some of the tins were contaminated with spores of the bacteria *Clostridium botulinum:* These bacteria cause fatal botulism in the eater unless the food is thoroughly boiled before consumption. Another poison was contained in the tins: The lead that sealed the seams and tops of the tin (enriched with arsenic to enhance the bonding properties) had leached into the food.

The potential loss of so much of the three-year supply of food was a serious setback. Forty percent of the provisions had been preserved in these tin cans; there was no way of telling how much of what remained was good. However, there was not any thought of turning back.

The spring of 1846 came early, and the summer promised to be unusually warm. By July the expedition managed to move on through Barrow Strait and turned into Peel Sound, sailing due south with moderate resistance from the scattered, receding ice. As Franklin approached what his maps indicated to be a peninsula named King William Land—but in fact was King William *Island*—he knew that he had already passed through half of the uncharted waters of the Northwest Passage. Ahead, a mere 200 miles, lay the northern Canadian coast (already mapped by Thomas Simpson) and open water to the Bering Strait. Proceeding into Victoria Strait to the west of King William Island rather than entering the narrow passage to the east, the *Erebus* and the

Stephan Goldner's Patent Preserved Provisions ⟿

Stephan Goldner was one of many London contractors who supplied food provisions for voyages made by ships of the Royal Navy. Usually the voyages were of short duration—three to six months. When the Admiralty requested bids for provisions for Sir John Franklin's Arctic voyage that would last for three years, Goldner wasted no time in presenting a bid for a contract that would make him a wealthy man. His bid was less than half that of his lowest competitor, and he was awarded the contract. He was able to fulfill the contract by defrauding the Royal Navy on almost every particular specified. Instead of a variety of 16 soups, every can was a mush of half-frozen, rotten, winter-stored root vegetables, half-cooked. He labeled these cans variously: carrot, ox tail, veal, even real turtle. An advertised 15 varieties of beef all turned out to be six-month-old salt beef—if it was in fact beef. It might have been horse or even mule. Goldner threw bones, gristle, intestines, feet, and whatever else came to hand, into the cooking pots. He added water to everything and thickened it with alum, a chemical agent. There was sand in the sugar and gravel in the soup. Everything was undercooked, despite his "patented process," and it is believed that the deadly botulinum contamination was present in almost every can.

Goldner delivered the bulk of the huge order just two days before Franklin left London. The Admiralty was so relieved to finally receive the order that they made no inspection of any of the canned foodstuffs.

It was years before Goldner's villainy was brought to light. By 1852, as retribution for his misdeeds seemed inevitable, he apparently left London and was never heard of again.

Sir John Franklin's ships, the *Erebus* and the *Terror*, became frozen in ice near King William Island after traveling through ever-enlarging ice floes much like the ones shown here. *(Library of Congress, Prints and Photographs Division [LC-USZ62-101009])*

Terror found themselves in one of the most treacherous, dangerous areas of the Arctic where they confronted an ever-thickening, turbulent sea filled with larger and larger ice floes. For a brief time, days perhaps, Franklin might have retreated, but retreat was not an option for a man like Franklin. With the steam engine fired to the maximum he drove on, certain that the ice would thin out as he progressed south. Soon the floes became solid ice five, then six, then seven inches thick. The two ships slowed, then stopped, powerless and held fast by the ice.

The *Erebus* and the *Terror* were held 15 miles off the northwest shore of King William Island, near Victoria Point. They were squarely in the path of the "ice stream," the unrelenting gale force wind that sweeps down from the North Pole. In the distance, through the mist and snow, the horizon of King William Island could be seen, although it would prove to offer no comfortable haven. The island had little or no wildlife and no vegetation larger than the frozen moss that clung to the black rock already buried under snow. Furthermore, as the explorers soon found out, the journey of 15 miles over the ice to the island was a nightmarish three-day trip; the return was even worse, in the teeth of the 40-mile-per-hour wind. Walking, let alone pulling a sledge with tent, fuel, and provisions was extremely difficult. Explor-

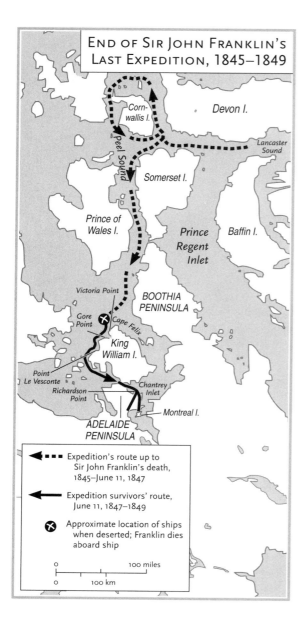

END OF SIR JOHN FRANKLIN'S
LAST EXPEDITION, 1845–1849

Corn-
wallis I.

Devon I.

Peel Sound

Lancaster
Sound

Somerset I.

Prince of
Wales I.

Prince
Regent
Inlet

Baffin I.

Victoria Point

BOOTHIA
PENINSULA

Gore
Point

Cape Felix

King
William I.

Point
Le Vesconte

Richardson
Point

Chantrey
Inlet

Montreal I.

ADELAIDE
PENINSULA

◀▪▪▪ Expedition's route up to
Sir John Franklin's death,
1845–June 11, 1847

◀━━ Expedition survivors' route,
June 11, 1847–1849

✕ Approximate location of ships
when deserted; Franklin dies
aboard ship

0   100 miles
0   100 km

atory parties were sent out, nonetheless, to see if perhaps the water was open to the south. It was not. The pack ice in which the ships were held grew thicker—10 feet, in places 14 feet. By September the party realized that they must spend this second winter trapped in the frozen water of the Victoria Strait.

The future seemed far less bright than it had a year earlier. Food supplies were running short; even precious freshwater was a problem since there was not enough fuel left to melt ice and keep the sleeping quarters warm. The mysterious disease had returned, men died, and more rotten canned meat had to be discarded. There was still some lemon juice left, but the crew hated to take their daily allotment, and the juice was undoubtedly losing its potency. Here and there a case of scurvy broke out. All the while the invisible lead poison from the lead-sealed tins was slowly breaking down red blood cells, creating a general weakness and fatigue, clouding the judgment of officers and men.

The winter of 1846 was a hard one, but the Franklin party was sustained by the belief that the summer of 1847 would bring release from the ice. As the new year began, exploratory parties made ready to search to the south and west for open water. Sledges were built and supplies packed for the short expeditions that hopefully would find some evidence that a breakup of ice was on the way. By April the ice master was in his crow's nest daily to scan with telescope the miles and miles of surrounding solid ice. There were no breaks, no signs of the blue water that would indicate a thaw was beginning. If anything, there was more ice packing, jamming in, creating even rougher, unnavigable ice fields. By June 1847 it was clear that there would be no early spring, no warm summer, no release from imprisonment.

On June 11, Franklin died, probably from scurvy but in any case from the effects of the poor diet and harsh climate on a 61-year-old man. The loss of the commander who was respected and beloved by the men deepened the dark foreboding mood that pervaded both ships. They wondered how they could survive another 12 months. Already the food supply was dangerously low. Captain Crozier, now in command (evidently Captain Fitzjames conceded to Crozier's age and experience), had ordered 6/4 rations: Six men now shared the amount of food previously given to four men. The allotment of rum and tobacco stayed the same, but even water was rationed to a few swallows a day per man. There was no water for washing and shaving; the crew's quarters had long since become unspeakably filthy. Rats, as hungry as the crew, had become desperately bold and no longer afraid of humans; they prowled the hold, eating into everything that was not sealed in metal.

Outside, the ice stream took its toll on the immobile, vulnerable ships. The *Terror,* caught in broken ice floes constantly moving with the gale winds above and currents below, began to drift away. On the *Erebus,* the sailors listened nightly to the creaking and cracking of the ship's timbers against the background of the never-ending gale winds sweeping down from the Pole. The *Erebus* was breaking up. There was little possibility that the ship would be seaworthy even if the ice left.

At some time during the terrible winter of 1847–48, Captain Crozier made the decision to abandon the ships as early in the spring as the weather permitted. Crozier decided to strike out for the Canadian mainland, to the nearest point due south, the Adelaide Peninsula. He had heard that game and fish were abundant there. After the party had regained their strength over the summer of 1848 Crozier planned to find Back's Great Fish River and follow it upstream to the Great Slave Lake (in the Canadian Northwest Territories) where

there were trading posts. Crozier knew there were a number of things to be done in preparation for the dramatic step of leaving the shelter of the ships. By this time he had discovered that King William Land was actually an island, so it would be necessary to take boats on the march to get off the island. And of course, boats would be needed for the voyage up Great Fish River. Early in the winter Crozier selected seven boats to transport. The boats, none larger than 24 feet in length, would be loaded with provisions, clothing, and tools. In order to haul the boats, Crozier had massive sledges built (out of oak from the ships). The boat-sledges, when loaded, weighed at least 1,500 pounds.

In March 1848, Crozier began to ferry boats, sledges, food, clothing, tools, stoves, and all necessities from the ships to the shore of King William Island. This was heart-breaking work for the men, who by this time were undernourished and ridden with scurvy and lead sickness. Back and forth from the ships they toiled in the constant wind and temperatures rarely above −40° Fahrenheit. Finally, a mountain of cargo sat on the rock and ice that was the shore of the island. It took 10 men to budge one of the sledges an inch: They were facing pressure ridges (masses of piled-up ice), pockets of six-feet-deep snow, and a terrain that a healthy, strong man with no load might pick his way through at a rate of three miles a day. They had to move this mass 1,000 miles. One man, Harry Peglar, wrote in his journal: "We have some very hard ground to heave." Everyone knew that this march, this journey of desperation, was the only chance of survival.

THE FINAL MONTHS

On April 25, 1848, Lieutenant Graham Gore placed a report of the mission in a cairn, or pile of rocks, at Victoria Point. A note from Captains Fitzjames and Crozier was included in the report and read as follows:

> 28th April 1848. H.M.S ships Terror and Erebus were deserted on the 22nd April . . . having been beset since 12th September 1846 The officers and crew consisting of 105 souls under the command of Captain F.R.M. Crozier . . . and start on tomorrow 26th for Back's Fish River.

On April 26, the expedition that had originally numbered 135, now down to 105, headed south. Much of the mountain of supplies stockpiled on the shore was abandoned. One week later, after progressing only six miles, another pile of goods was left behind. This time many of the items were personal and nonessential: curtain rods, sets of silver tableware, fancy dress clothes, a portable lightning rod, and a mahogany writing desk. At least one man was dying each day: exposure, gangrene from frostbite, scurvy, food poisoning, and starvation each took its toll. As the group followed the shoreline of King William Island south, it tried to deal with hummocks of ice, pressure ridges, slushy shore ice, and deep snow. Two hundred yards in five hours was unusually good progress.

In desperation, Crozier divided the expedition into those who were unfit and those who could still pull the one and a half ton sledge-boats. Those who were fit went on, promising to return with help; the infirm were to struggle north back to the ships, or at least to the abandoned supplies left on shore at Victoria Point. Some of these unfortunates fell down as they walked or pulled a sledge-boat that held their meager supplies. At first, the dead were attended to, with cairns of rock, if possible; at the end they were left where they fell. The last men died with their sledge-boat: Two inside as if asleep, and one face down beside the forever stalled burden.

By mid-August 1848, the main party had finally reached the southern tip of King William Island. There must have been no more than 35 left in this party; Captain Fitzjames had evidently died by this time, but none of Fitzjames's remains or belongings have ever been found. The survivors were still almost 100 miles from the mouth of Back's River. There was no food, for they had neither seen nor killed game. Here, at Booth Point, the retreat would end for all if food could not be obtained. Crozier was forced to a decision: life or death. He decided to cannibalize the dead. Discoveries made in 1981 show how the surgeon's saw and scalpel were used with precision to render human corpses into food for the living. Every part was used, down to the nutritious marrow in the bones.

Starvation, for the moment, was averted. Crozier's party crossed the 23-mile ice of Simpson Strait to the Adelaide Peninsula and settled for the winter at Starvation Cove. They were given some help by Inuit in the winter of 1848, but the native people soon moved on. They could not possibly feed 30 starving men—especially hungry, armed men who were carrying strips of dried human flesh.

In 1849, some of the survivors reached Montreal Island, located very near the mouth of Back's River. But for some reason—and by some means—some of the men from Crozier's party returned to the *Erebus* and the *Terror.* They were visited by Inuit aboard the *Erebus* during the winter of 1849–50. Sometime in 1850 the broken *Terror* began to drift further south in the ice of Victoria Strait. The *Erebus,* lay wrecked on its side in the ice just off shore at King William Island.

There was no sheltering place now for the remnants of Franklin's party still with Crozier. They wandered mindlessly, scurvy-ridden skeletons. The Inuit watched the dreadful march as man after man walked to his death. One explorer, perhaps the last, died of scurvy and starvation as he walked. In his pack were 12 pounds of chocolate, found with his frozen remains.

When Crozier crossed Simpson Strait, he may or may not have realized that he was completing the last undiscovered part of the Northwest Passage. If Crozier was aware, he must have felt that the cost of his success was high. But whatever the thoughts of the last survivors of the Franklin expedition, all contact with the world outside had now been cut off. Sir John Franklin and all the members of his expedition had effectively vanished from the known bounds of the Earth, and the search for the Northwest Passage had once again come to a dead end. Yet as Franklin himself had concluded in his published account of his earlier voyages,

> It is, moreover, pleasing to reflect that the loss of life which has occurred in the prosecution of these discoveries does not exceed the average number of deaths in the same population at home under circumstances most favourable. And it is sincerely to be hoped that Great Britain will not relax her efforts until the question of a northwest passage has been satisfactorily set at rest.

2

THE POLAR REGIONS

In modern times, the term *polar* refers both to scientifically defined areas and to regions that are more generally characterized as "polar." To geographers, the North Polar Region, or the Arctic, is the area from the North Pole (90° N) to the Arctic Circle (66°33' N). The South Polar Region, or the Antarctic, is the area from the South Pole (90° S) to the Antarctic Circle (66°33' S). The circles represent the farthest point from either pole where there is a full 24 hours of direct sunlight on a midsummer day. In the case of Antarctica, this occurs in December; in the Arctic, this happens in June.

Nature, however, does not draw such a strict line, and when it comes to the history of exploration, both senses of *polar* must be considered. Explorers who sought to reveal and master the geographers' strict polar regions inevitably had to spend a fair amount of time in the bordering seas and lands. The conditions that they confronted there were often every bit as challenging as those within the circles. Water, which was permanently frozen at the poles, could become, in the subpolar regions, open water overnight, trapping the unwary traveler.

THE ARCTIC DISCOVERED

People have been living within the Arctic Circle for several thousand years, but for much of that time they did not have any communication with peoples outside their region. In the ancient civilizations centered around the Mediterranean, peoples' ideas about the North Pole region were completely speculative, often based on myths. Rumors of a cold region far to the north must have reached some of these ancients; mariners and merchants would have met men who had had some experience with the polar region.

Probably the oldest known account of contact with either polar region was that of the voyage by Pytheas, a Greek from Massalia (present-day Marseilles, in France), about 325 B.C. He referred to an island north of Britain—"Thule,"—and a frozen sea, but exactly what land Thule was or how far north it was could only be imagined, considering how little geography of the Earth was known. The ancient Greeks were nonetheless quite curious about the unknown north and gave it the name Arktos, "the bear," the same name for the constellation that appears in the northern sky and that today is still known as the Great Bear. Some Greeks believed that people called the Hyperboreans (those beyond the north wind) were living in a paradise so far north that they escaped the harsh climate associated with the Arctic.

In the centuries that followed, little true knowledge of the Arctic region was gained. Maps of the later Greeks and Romans, for instance, continued to be based heavily on fantasy and speculation rather than exploration and knowledge. The Roman historian Tactitus (ca. A.D. 55–120) described people of the north who were probably those known today as Lapps, but few people would have known of such writings. In the 10th and 11th centuries, however, this changed for some Europeans when Norwegian Vikings moved westward, first to Iceland and then to Greenland.

About the year 1000, a few even briefly settled a land to the west that they named Vinland, now believed to have been the tip of Newfoundland. The Vikings brought tales of wild, hostile people back to Iceland and Norway. They told also of a climate warm and habitable to the south and impossibly cold to the north. All of this was set down in long accounts known as sagas, which record the explorations of the Norwegian Vikings in the 10th, 11th, and 12th centuries. Few people outside the Viking community, however, knew of these sagas.

In 1555, Olaus Magnus, the Catholic archbishop of Sweden, published a treatise called *A History of the Northern Peoples,* which drew in part on Viking accounts of travels in the New World—that is, Greenland and Vinland. This account was the basis of European knowledge about the Arctic for the next century. Meanwhile, by the end of the 16th century, exploration and an interest in geography and cartography had vastly improved Euro-

peans' sense of what the Earth looked like. In 1595, a comprehensive atlas of the world, the work of the great Belgian mapmaker Gerardus Mercator, contained a chart of the Arctic. The chart asserted that under the North Pole "lies a bare rock in the midst of the sea. Its circumference is almost 33 French miles, and it is all of magnetic stone." Mercator also described a giant whirlpool at the Pole into which poured all the polar waters.

The reference to "magnetic stone" reflected the fact that by this time mariners knew that the magnetic needles of their compasses pointed to the North Magnetic Pole when in the Northern Hemisphere and to the South Magnetic Pole when in the Southern Hemisphere. Since about 1450, too, some were beginning to realize that the North Magnetic Pole was not exactly the same as the "true north"—the imaginary point at the opposite ends of the Earth where all the lines of longitude meet. The mixture of fact, near fact, and pure fiction exemplified by Mercator's chart characterizes the state of knowledge about the North Polar Region circa 1600. Speculation and guesswork had not and could not provide accurate information about the geography of the Arctic. Exploration of the area by ship or overland would still be required to solve the mystery of what lay inside the Arctic Circle and at the North Pole.

The search for sea routes linking the Atlantic and Pacific Oceans across the top of North America (the Northwest Passage) and across the top of Eurasia (the Northeast Passage) as well as the journeys of whalers and sealers into unknown northern waters brought about the discovery and the exploration of the Arctic. By the mid-1800s, the Arctic Circle around the North Pole was complete, but what was inside was still largely a mystery.

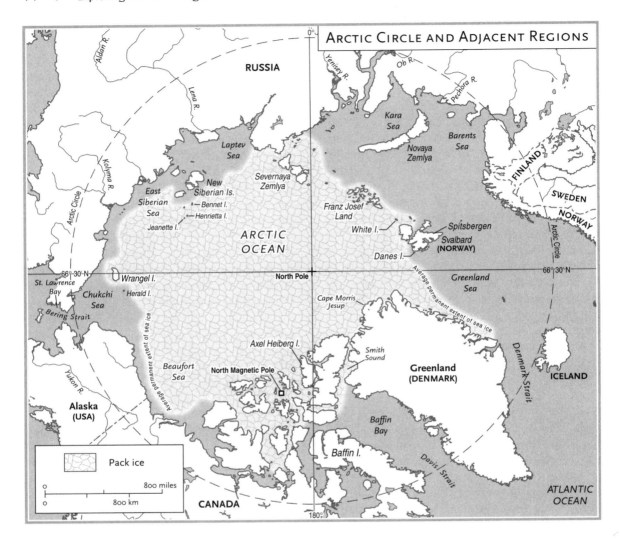

ARCTIC CIRCLE AND ADJACENT REGIONS

WITHIN THE ARCTIC CIRCLE

It would be several decades from the mid-1800s before the mystery of what was inside the Arctic Circle was solved. The answer was one simple word: *ice*. Here and there within the Arctic Circle were frozen areas that sometimes melted in the two months of summer, and sometimes, but rarely, there were sections of the Arctic that were open water the year round. But mostly there was ice because the Arctic is composed mainly of the Arctic Ocean. The ice pack on the Arctic Ocean is not one smooth sheet of ice; rather, it is an uneven mass of floes on top of floes and pressure ridges, which force pieces of ice upward at angles, creating a surface that can be traversed only with great difficulty. In the summer, leads (channels of water) may open up creating streams that may be a yard wide or a mile across. For an Arctic traveler pulling a sledge, a lead presents great difficulty and deadly danger. The Arctic pack ice, always on the move, flows generally east, over the Pole, and then southward down the east coast of Greenland. The pack, at times up to 12 feet thick, begins to break up into smaller and smaller pieces, as it floats into warmer water.

The geographic North Pole is also under moving pack ice. This means that an explorer camped on top of the North Pole one day, might on the next day be two or three miles away from the Pole, having floated along in the polar wind and the current of the frozen sea.

Surrounding the frozen Arctic Ocean are landmasses. They are, starting with the two-thirds of Greenland that lies within the Arctic Circle and moving eastward, the northern tip of Sweden, Norway, and Finland; the entire northern coast of Russia and three major groups of islands off the Russian coast; the northeastern part of Alaska; the northern rim of Canada; the entire Canadian Archipelago; and most of Baffin Island.

All of these lands border on seas that, whatever their local names, are extensions of the Arctic Ocean. Not all of these waters are frozen the year round. In fact, if explorers moved around the southernmost part of the Arctic region, they would find plenty of open water, especially in the summer, except in the Canadian Archipelago where the multitude of islands serve to hold and protect the winter ice. This situation is mainly why the Northeast

Ice breakers can be either attached to ships or free standing, similar to these off the northern coast of Russia. *(Library of Congress, Prints and Photographs Division [LC-DIG-prok-10613])*

Despite the harshness of the environment as evidenced by the bleached skull in the center of this image, this typical tundra scene demonstrates the variety of plant life that thrives in the Arctic. *(Bureau of Land Management)*

Passage through the ocean at the top of Eurasia is navigable while the Northwest Passage through the ocean across the top of North America is not. In summer and in winter with ice breakers, the entire north Russian coast is traversable.

The weather moderates from the region of the Pole to the Arctic Circle and further south. The lowest temperature recorded in the Arctic is –90° Fahrenheit in Siberia and a few degrees lower in Alaska and northern Greenland. But along the Arctic Circle the temperature is surprisingly warm in the brief summer months of July and August, reaching 50° Fahrenheit and higher in some places. Under these conditions, there is a wide variety of plant life—more than 400 kinds of higher plants—and animal life—including hoards of insects.

Much of the animal life of the Arctic lives in or is dependent on the water. Water is the environment of the polar region, and the water is warmer than the air. Polar land animals mainly are the musk ox, the caribou, the arctic fox, the arctic wolf, the hare, and the lemming. The polar bear is as at home in the water as on land, although it obtains almost all its food from the water. There is a variety of birds: geese, ducks, auks, and gulls; most of these migrate south in the winter. The snowy owl, the arctic raven, and the ptarmigan remain in the Arctic year round.

The Arctic Ocean abounds with life, from plankton to the calanus (a shrimplike creature) and fish. The arctic char is in abundance, and in the warmer regions of the Arctic there are cod, halibut, salmon, and the arctic shark. At least five kinds of whales inhabit the Arctic waters, as do walruses and many varieties of seals. Experts believe that the seal has been the mainstay of Inuit existence since the original migration to the far northern regions.

PEOPLE OF THE ARCTIC

More than 1 million people live in and just below the Arctic Circle; the majority of these hardy folk live in Siberia or in Inuit settlements in Alaska and Canada. The indigenous people who inhabit the Arctic fall mainly into the following groups: the Sami, the Chukchi, the Inuit, and the Athapascans.

The Sami inhabit the Arctic regions of Norway, Sweden, the Russian Kola Peninsula, and Lapland. The ancestors of the Sami occupied these coastal areas 10,000 years ago; they were always hunters and fishers, and over the years also became known as reindeer herders. The Chukchi live in the most remote part of Siberia on the east extension of the Chukot Peninsula; the terrain is mountainous and the weather there is perhaps the coldest in all of the Arctic. The Chukchi live both by hunting and fishing and by the domestication of reindeer.

Inuit, which means "the people," has generally replaced the term *Eskimo,* which for most indigenous people has a derogatory connotation. (The word is derived from the French *esquimaux,* which was probably adapted from an Algonquian word for "eaters of raw flesh.") The Inuit inhabit the Arctic and subarctic from the east coast of Greenland to the Alaskan side of the Bering Strait. The first Inuit, it is thought, migrated to their present locations from Siberia and central Asia, about 5,000 years ago. They were hunters and fishers, as are the descendants today; being seminomadic, they moved to where game and seals were more plentiful.

Archaeologists believe that the first Athapascans crossed the Bering Strait into Alaska

Many Inuit have traditionally built igloos, or shelters made of large blocks of ice, such as this one on Baffin Island off the northern coast of Canada. *(Library of Congress, Prints and Photographs Division [LC-USZ62-103524])*

Cultural Conventions of Arctic Inhabitants ⌒

Dividing the indigenous peoples of the Arctic into distinct groups is an uncertain and questionable process. But for convenience the Arctic region can be divided into two areas, and the residents can be assigned to two groups. The eastern sector—that is, the Eurasian territory—is the dwelling place of the Sami, the Yakut, the Even, the Chukchi, and the Koryak. In the Western Hemisphere, the peoples now dwelling from Alaska to Greenland are the Inuit, Yup'ik, Inupiaq, Alaska Natives, and Athapascans. (The Aleut inhabit the string of islands extending from Alaska and geographically outside the Arctic region.) One characteristic the eastern dwellers have in common is that they are all reindeer herders; the westerners are not. Except for that distinction, both groups tend to share many cultural conventions.

Most Arctic peoples used to be seminomadic (until the early part of the 20th century) because they had to move seasonally to where the food was. With no possibility of agriculture in the Arctic, the source of food was what could be obtained by hunting and fishing. Because the Inuit and other western peoples were constantly on the move, there was never any strong tribal organization: The social unit was the family or a group of several families, headed by a leader who was probably the best hunter or fisher or an effective shaman (spiritual leader).

The Arctic peoples of the period of European exploration shared a number of values or cultural attributes, and these characteristics appear to be the direct results of the difficult conditions of existence. First of all, they put great value on skill: This meant primarily skill in hunting, because providing food was the basis of continuing existence. Second, they put very little value on possessions. This trait led to a basic generosity and honesty. Giving things away, particularly food, demonstrated their success as skillful hunters and was a source of great pleasure to them. By the same token, they did not understand the concept of theft. How could it be bad to take something from another, since they would gladly give what they might have if another wanted it? Many a European explorer criticized the Arctic inhabitants' ways, but the indigenous people could never understand the Europeans' attachment to things.

A third value of the Arctic peoples was the total commitment to the welfare of the group by each individual. It would be unthinkable for an Arctic individual or family to eat a meal while a neighbor had no food. All the necessities of life were thought of as communal property. This led to conduct that often struck Europeans as extreme. If a hunter had to go away on a long hunting trip, a friend was encouraged to "use" his wife while he was away. Children, although always

about 10,000 years ago; they moved inland and stayed there, becoming hunters and living in villages in a fairly stationary way. Eventually the Athapascans migrated above and below the Arctic Circle in Alaska, to the Yukon and the Northwest Territories and south into what

loved by their parents, could be "given" to a childless couple to help them survive. In times of hardship, girl babies and beloved elders might be abandoned to die for the welfare of the larger group.

A fourth cultural trait of the Arctic peoples was that of apparent passivity: Emotions should not be shown, and the general mood of the group should not be disturbed by the emotions of the individual, no matter how deeply felt. Anger at an offspring's neglect of the dog team, for example, would be expressed in this way: "One feels that the dogs have worked hard today and are probably hungry now." Underlying all these peoples' social relationships was a true regard and respect for others, yet Europeans, not understanding the Arctic inhabitants' cultural convictions, and applying their own standards, were often critical of their behavior.

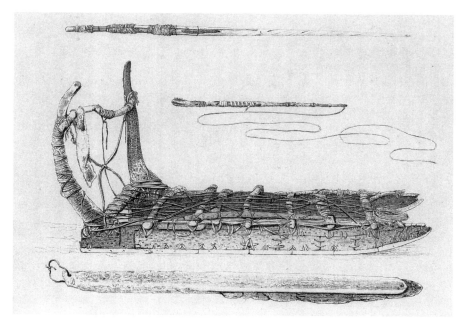

Published in an early 1800s book, this illustration shows tools—a spear, a whip, a dog sled made of bone, and a knife—that were likely quite important to an Inuit family as they hunted for food. *(Library of Congress, Prints and Photographs Division [LC-USZ62-87314])*

is now the western Canadian provinces. These Athapascans today prefer to call themselves Dene, meaning "the people." Other Athapas-cans moved down into the American Southwest; these are the people known as the Navajo and Apache.

Crafted very carefully and insulated with animal skins, igloos, such as the one shown here, were often quite comfortable inside. *(Library of Congress, Prints and Photographs Division [LOT 11453-5, no. 14])*

The peoples who live throughout the Arctic region speak many different languages that linguists group into several families, but most of the languages are quite distinct from one another. Although it is assumed that the languages spoken across the North American Arctic must have originally come from those spoken in Asia, linguists are unable to agree on any direct relationships. The main languages spoken by the non-Athapascan peoples who live across North America are grouped as Inuit and Yupik, and within each group there are many variations. Because there is a common root, two strangers might be able to communicate, if only in a simple and basic way. In all cases, the languages spoken by Arctic peoples are expressive and capable of complex ideas when the subject is a matter that concerns these peoples' basic interests.

ANTARCTICA DISCOVERED

Long before Antarctica was ever seen by the human eye, it existed as a hypothesis of certain ancient Greeks who decided that a great landmass must lie far south to counterbalance the landmass of Eurasia to the north. The great Greek philosophers Plato and Aristotle were among those who believed that the Earth was a round sphere and therefore that certain laws of symmetry or balance had to apply. Theopompos, a Greek historian who flourished about 350 B.C., was perhaps the first to set down in writing the notion of a vast "dry land" that bordered the southern ocean. Plato was among the first to dub the inhabitants of the place "antipodes" (opposite feet). In some Greek writings, the land itself is referred to as the Antipodes, but other Greeks began to refer to the land as Antarktos, "opposite the Arctic."

The Romans adopted this notion of a southern land and named it Terra Australis Incognita (unknown southern land), and that is how it remained for many centuries to come, a vast continent that lay below Africa, India, China, and South America. About the year A.D. 150, the most important astronomer and geographer of his time in the Eastern Hemisphere, Claudius Ptolemy, a Greek living in the Roman-controlled city of Alexandria, Egypt, produced a map of the world that gave prominent space to this Terra Australis Incognita. Although the original map of Ptolemy did not survive, copies of it were made, and it remained the most influential map of the world until about 1400. The Catholic Church opposed the idea of a place and people so far removed from biblical activity as heretical; for example in 741, a priest was excommunicated for teaching about the Antipodes.

It was not until the 15th century and later, however, that nautical exploration and actual observation and experience became the basis for cartography and speculation about the southern continent. After such voyages as those of Marco Polo, Christopher Columbus, and Vasco da Gama, it was impossible for the church fathers to continue to insist that the Earth was not round and that places not in the Bible could not exist. After Ferdinand Magellan's expedition returned from its voyage around the world in 1519–22, the possibility of Terra Australis Incognita became very real to Europeans. Furthermore, the Maori who inhabited New Zealand by this time had tales about a large "white land" to the south, suggesting that some among them had at least caught a glimpse of Antarctica.

During the two centuries following 1550, explorers began to search for the southern continent. Exploration is difficult if the object of search is completely unknown as to size, whereabouts, or even whether it might be land or water. Furthermore, there was no convenient jumping-off point: The nearest land to the so-called hidden continent (as far as the explorer knew) were the tips of South America and Africa, but these places had no settled populations and no ports where supplies could be restocked. Just getting into position for a search involved a long expedition of 10,000 miles from Europe. One early expedition that encountered great difficulty added some information about the southern seas: In 1578 Sir Francis Drake, while sailing around the globe, discovered Cape Horn and the archipelago off the tip of South America. However, looking south from Tierra del Fuego into the empty expanse of ocean (which he named Drake Passage) he declared that no land existed in that direction.

In 1673 Antonio de La Roché, a London merchant, undertook an expedition to Peru; on his return voyage in 1675, rounding the tip of South America, he was blown off course by a terrible storm. Inadvertently, he discovered South Georgia Island and Clerk Rocks, far out in the South Atlantic but well north of Antarctica. The latter island, clouded by mist and fog, surrounded by icebergs, and rising 1,000 feet from the sea with snow-capped peaks, made La Roché believe that he had sighted the coast of the southern land. He had not, but his reports gave a strong impression of what conditions must prevail in that remote sector of the world: wind-swept, desolate emptiness surrounded by wind-torn hostile seas.

In 1738, a French naval officer, Jean Bouvet de Lozier, left France on a mission to discover the "Southern Lands," believed by him to lie south of the tip of Africa. From there, some 1,000 miles south, he did discover Bouvet Island (called the most isolated island on Earth) but was unable to land there because of stormy seas. Bouvet eventually reached 54°40'S and met thickening ice. He followed the edge of the pack ice for 1,500 miles but saw no land. He returned to France in 1739, convinced that the large number of icebergs he saw indicated the existence of a glacier-filled landmass somewhere further south within the pack ice.

Explorers were beginning to zero in on Terra Australis. On his second voyage (1772–74), English explorer James Cook and the *Resolution* circumnavigated the globe at high southern latitudes, reaching 71°10', the farthest south recorded to that time, and crossing the Antarctic Circle three times. He proved that the southern continent must lie within the ice pack and observed in his journal that "the world will derive no benefit from it." When Cook finished his expedition he had sailed through 20,000 miles of unknown oceans, facing weather and storm-ridden seas that constituted some of the worst conditions to be found on the planet. His

Accompanying James Cook on his second Pacific voyage, artist William Hodges captured the beauty and wonder of the expedition's discoveries in paintings. This engraving, based on one of Hodges's paintings, was included in Cook's two-volume account of his voyages. *(Library of Congress, Prints and Photographs Division [LC-USZ62-77398])*

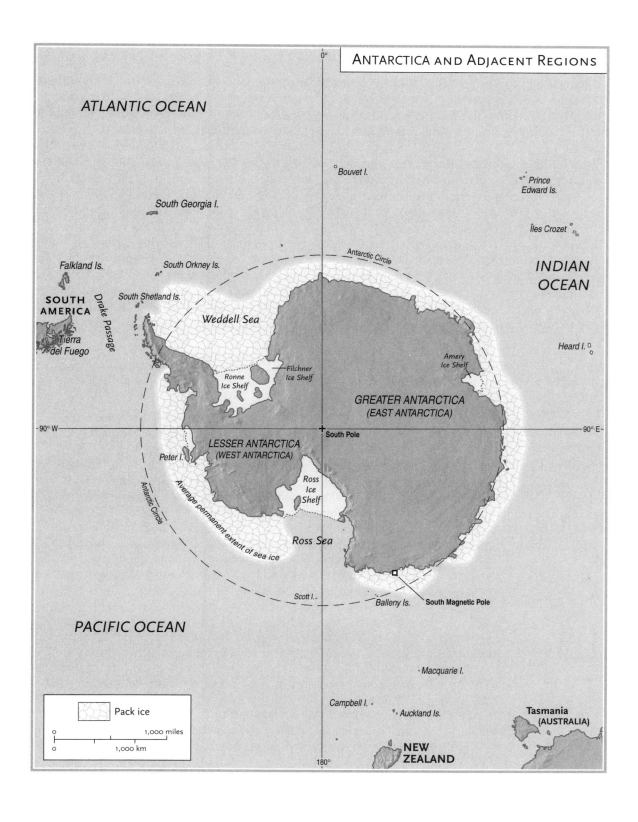

ANTARCTICA AND ADJACENT REGIONS

ATLANTIC OCEAN

Bouvet I.

Prince Edward Is.

South Georgia I.

Îles Crozet

INDIAN OCEAN

Antarctic Circle

Falkland Is.

South Orkney Is.

SOUTH AMERICA

Drake Passage

South Shetland Is.

Weddell Sea

Heard I.

Tierra del Fuego

Ronne Ice Shelf

Filchner Ice Shelf

Amery Ice Shelf

GREATER ANTARCTICA (EAST ANTARCTICA)

90° W

South Pole

90° E

Peter I.

LESSER ANTARCTICA (WEST ANTARCTICA)

Ross Ice Shelf

Average permanent extent of sea ice

Antarctic Circle

Ross Sea

Scott I.

Balleny Is.

South Magnetic Pole

PACIFIC OCEAN

Macquarie I.

Campbell I.

Auckland Is.

Tasmania (AUSTRALIA)

Pack ice

0   1,000 miles

0   1,000 km

NEW ZEALAND

0°

180°

voyage of circumnavigation has been called the greatest exploration by sea ever undertaken, but his failure to find the hidden continent served to discourage similar attempts for a while.

It also had another effect: It encouraged sealer and whaling expeditions to move into the region in ever-increasing numbers. It is estimated that by 1820 there were 50 British and U.S. ships in the vicinity of the Antarctic Circle in search of the seals and whales by which a fortune could be made overnight. It was probably an unknown British or U.S. sealing ship that first caught sight of Antarctica; unable to get closer because of the pack ice, the seal hunters moved off in search of islands teeming with the valuable quarry. The Americans claim that the first to see the Antarctic Peninsula was Nathaniel B. Palmer who sailed along its west coast in 1820; the British claim that their Edward Bransfield sighted the peninsula still earlier in 1820. Whichever is the case, it is certain that in 1820 both of these skippers were more concerned with seals than with discovering Terra Australis.

A number of sightings and landings occurred in the 19th century, as explorers and hunters penetrated deeper into the pack ice barrier around Antarctica. In 1821, Thaddeus von Bellingshausen, a German in the Russian navy, sailing in the sea off Antarctica that would be named after him, sighted two

The Wilkes Expedition 〜

The U.S. South Seas Exploring Expedition of 1838–42, headed by Lieutenant Charles Wilkes, is one of the most fascinating and important in the history of exploration. A squadron of six sailing ships with 346 men, including scientists and artists, made up the expedition. The group journeyed first from the east coast of the United States down to the southern Pacific where it mapped 1,500 miles of the Antarctic coast. The expedition then moved on and mapped 800 miles of the Pacific Northwest coast. In total it surveyed 280 Pacific islands, produced 180 charts of hitherto unknown waters for use by mariners, and returning home after four years having sailed 87,000 miles, with the loss of two ships and 28 of the men. This certainly qualifies as one of the most ambitious expeditions of all time, yet neither it nor its commander get much recognition compared, say, to the Lewis and Clark expedition. There are several reasons why. The expedition had been commissioned by the Democratic president Martin Van Buren, but when it returned, a Whig, John Tyler, was president and was not anxious to publicize Wilkes's achievements. In fact, the secretary of the navy had Wilkes and some of his officers tried on charges of misconduct; Wilkes was found guilty of harsh flogging of some of the crew. Wilkes was in fact his own worst enemy. He was an erratic, insecure, and despotic leader and ended up antagonizing virtually all who sailed with him as well as others. Some Antarctic explorers seemed to delight in discrediting him by emphasizing errors he had inevitably made in his reports. It is sad but perhaps fitting that the major memorial to this man is the remote and frozen section of Antarctica whose coast he surveyed, now known as Wilkes Land.

islands that he thought were the mainland; they were eventually named for two Russian czars, Peter I and Alexander I. Also in 1821, John Davis, an American seal hunter, entered Hughes Bay on the tip of Antarctic Peninsula and sent crew members ashore on February 7. Between 1821 and 1824, James Weddell, a British seal hunter, steamed to 74°15' S and discovered and named the Weddell Sea.

Between 1838 and 1842, Lieutenant Charles Wilkes led a U.S. Navy expedition that sailed into the Indian Ocean and throughout much of the Pacific Ocean. In 1839, he headed south to the still-unnamed land and then sailed along some 1,500 miles of the coast, establishing once and for all that this was a vast landmass, not just a number of islands. Wilkes is now credited with both naming this land Antarctica and proving that it is a continent. In 1840, Jules-Sébastien-César Dumont d'Urville, a French explorer, sighted land and bestowed the name of his wife, Adélie, on both the region and the penguins he found there. This phase of Antarctic exploration climaxed with the expedition of the English explorer James Clark Ross, who between 1841 and 1843 discovered and named a great number of natural features along the coast of Antarctica. When members of his expedition set foot on an offshore island that would eventually be named after him, the exploration of Antarctica entered a new chapter.

THE GEOGRAPHY OF ANTARCTICA

The continent of Antarctica is a roughly circular mass of ice positioned between the Atlantic, the Pacific, and the Indian Oceans. Its area is some 5.5 million square miles (compared to Australia's area of some 2.96 million

Icebergs, much of whose mass is hidden below the water's surface, contribute to the difficulties faced by Arctic and Antarctic explorers. *(Library of Congress, Prints and Photographs Division [LC-USZ62-69624])*

square miles). Surrounding it is the Southern Ocean, which lies between the 50th and 70th parallels; over this ocean an unimpeded windstorm blows almost constantly. On an average day, a force 8 gale—as indicated by the Beaufort scale, the standard for measuring

"Blasted Funny Wee Beggars" ⟿

Penguins have amused and amazed explorers in the southern regions from the 16th century to the present. Sailors with Ferdinand Magellan in 1520 called them "strange black geese" and were surprised that they could not fly. W. G. Burn Murdoch, a Scottish artist, painting the penguins in 1892, wrote in his account of the expedition that a Scottish sailor called them "blasted funny wee beggars." The penguin, beautifully graceful in the water, is much less so on land or ice. Its waddle is intensified by the fact that the penguin is, or seems to be, always off balance. Indeed, penguins are easily thrown off kilter by the slightest bump or irregularity in the ice or rock. After stumbling, they appear to glare at the tiny offending obstacle, adjust the egg they might be carrying on their foot, and swagger off.

Penguins are dubbed "flightless birds," but there was a time when they flew. Scientists believe that 60 million years ago, penguins had broad wings that have since evolved into the flippers that they now use for swimming. This very old species has adapted incredibly well to the climate and extreme conditions of the Southern Hemisphere. As the wings formed into flippers, the bones of the wings, once hollow, became solid; muscles developed to better propel the sleek body through the water at high speed. The white coloration in front and the dark back made the penguin less visible to its predators. An air-breathing mechanism developed that allowed the bird to stay underwater for up to 20 minutes while searching for its favorite food, the krill, tiny shrimplike marine creatures.

The body of the penguin is well protected against the antarctic cold. Two layers of feathers provide a first barrier against the cold and the wind. The top layer of feathers overlap to form a tight wind-breaking overcoat; the second layer of feathers have tufts of down at their base and this creates a layer of air next to the skin. Penguins have a gland that secretes oil with which they groom themselves, thus making their feathers waterproof. Inside the skin there is an inch or two of fat, protecting the inner organs from any cold that might have gotten through the outer defenses. When the long antarctic night is really cold in the depths of winter, a large group of penguins will form a tightly packed oval, huddling together for warmth. Those on the cold outside gradually migrate to the warm center and vice versa. Penguins are not really threatened by the cold and never freeze to death; in fact, they are more bothered by the mild days of summer because their cold-protection systems are so efficient.

Breeding customs vary from one species of penguin to another, but most penguins build nests in communal areas occupied by mothers and their young

winds, from 0 (calm) to 12 (hurricane)— sweeps clockwise around the entire landmass; on a bad day the wind can reach 115 miles per hour; on a calm day there are 15-foot swells; when the weather is bad there are waves that are 50 feet from trough to summit. Most of the

called rookeries; the preferred materials are feathers and small, round stones. The female of some species lays only one egg; in other cases, two. Only one of the two eggs may be incubated, and the other kicked (literally) out of the nest. Generally, the king penguin does not even bother with a nest: The female goes off after laying an egg, and the male carries it on his feet, covered usually with a fringe of feathers, keeping it warm for the 55 days of incubation. When the female returns, having stuffed herself with all the fish and krill she can catch, she and her mate greet each other with elaborate bows and neck-stretching. Some species spend some time with the new offspring, but generally, the new little penguins are on their own after eight weeks or so from birth.

The curiosity and fearlessness of most penguins made them easy prey for the explorers who valued them for food and for the oil extracted from the layer of blubber. For a while whalers, running out of whales, hunted the king penguin for oil and even the penguin skin with its beautiful coat of fine feathers. The fashion of penguin feathers did not really catch on in Europe, so the penguin was left in peace to deal with its own natural enemy, the leopard seal.

Flightless and awkward on land, penguins have long fascinated Antarctic explorers. (Cyberphoto)

time there is fog and mist present: Moisture coats the intruding ship from deck to mast top with black ice, which is frozen mist and fog and unlike clear ice or frost is dark black because it has taken on the color of the surface beneath it. Spreading out hundreds of miles from the continent on all sides is thick pack ice, shifting and drifting and making further approach by ship impossible. For two months of the year this ring of ice is penetrable, with good navigation and luck. A ship caught in the pack will be crushed and pounded to destruction. The 19th-century English explorer James Clark Ross recounted his passage through the pack ice in his diary and concluded: "The awful grandeur of such a scene can be neither imagined or described."

Inside the gauntlet of stormy seas and ship-smashing ice lies the continent itself, a dome of ice covering 98 percent of its entire area and reaching as high as 14,000 feet at some points. Seen from a satellite, it appears to be a great white light as it reflects the sun (and its heat) back into the stratosphere. Antarctica has more than 90 percent of the world's ice and snow—more freshwater than in all the rest of the world combined. If the ice cap should somehow all melt, the rising world's oceans would cover New York City, London, Paris, and Rome, and half of the world's population would perish.

Under the ice is a landmass—or some scientists believe, a number of landmasses—pushed down below sea level by the weight of ice: 27,000 million billion tons. It has been measured that at one point, there are 15,580 feet of ice below sea level forming the base for the mile of ice that rises above the sea. Stretching across the continent are the Transantarctic Mountains, actually made up of several ranges; the highest peaks rise to some 16,000 feet. Many of the mountains are buried deep under the ice cap as are some lakes that remain unfrozen.

The ice of Antarctica is always on the move, inching by gravity downward to the edge of the ice mass in glaciers, narrow rivers of ice called tongues, and fast-moving ice streams. Sometimes the moving ice breaks off as it reaches the coast; more often it spreads out, still anchored to the land and forms ice shelves that eventually "calve," or break off into icebergs. The Ross Ice Shelf, for instance, grows out into the Southern Ocean at the rate of one-third of a mile per year. It has given birth to icebergs as large as 100 miles long, 10 miles wide, and hundreds of feet in depth. In the midst of the mountains of ice in the central regions lie the mysterious dry valleys, or oases—perpetually free of ice and much warmer than the surrounding mountains. Such valleys can be 40 miles long, five miles wide, and run 5,000 feet deep between the mountains.

The central plateau of Antarctica, although generally free of glaciers' movement, is the most hostile part of the continent: It is the driest part as well, with about two inches of snow per year. But here in the high interior is found the deepest cold and the most severe wind. A temperature of –135° Fahrenheit has been recorded at the South Pole—the lowest on Earth. Average temperatures on the plateau can vary from –30° to –60° Fahrenheit in the cold months, but the wind can make such cold more deadly. Australian Antarctic explorer Douglas Mawson described his winter in Adélie Land: "The wind blew non-stop for eight hours at an average speed of 107mph; gusts were recorded of over 150mph. . . . In these conditions it was possible to stand for no more than a few seconds."

LIFE ON ANTARCTICA

Indeed, the conditions at the South Polar Region make life on the continent itself all but impossible. Some varieties of grass and herbs grow on the Antarctic Peninsula. Lichens and mosses appear on exposed hillsides in the summer, but plants that have deep roots—trees and shrubs—simply cannot grow there. There are numerous species of insects, spiders, and microscopic creatures that live on the mosses and lichens. A wingless fly less than one-tenth of an inch long is the largest land animal on Antarctica except for the birds that put down there. The best known of these are the penguins, most of which nest on the islands on the edges of the continent itself. Among the birds that do live at least part of the year on Antarctica are skuas, cape pigeons, fulmars, and petrels. Arctic terns arrive each summer, having flown some 11,000 miles from their breeding grounds in the Arctic.

The ocean beneath and between the pack ice remains slightly above 32° Fahrenheit and is rich in phytoplankton. The shrimplike krill eat the plankton and are the real base of the food chain, providing sustenance for the penguins, the various species of birds, the several species of seals, and the several species of whales (including the blue whale, the largest animal that has ever lived). There are also hundreds of species of fish in the Southern Ocean.

Antarctica then, like the Arctic, is a land of ice, cold, wind and desolation. And both polar regions, as they were discovered and gradually explored, would prove to be as hostile to human presence as any place on the globe. The opening up of the two areas would eventually occur, and most of the myths and misconceptions about the polar regions would be exposed. The price of discovery would be high in terms of human suffering and life. The terrible climate and conditions of the Arctic and the Antarctic would not, however, discourage generations of explorers from their quest of discovery and enlightenment.

3

A NORTHWEST PASSAGE
The Search Begins

 After Christopher Columbus's successful voyage to North America in 1492, serious interest was generated in finding a passage through or north of this newly found landmass that would lead to Asia from the west. Five short years after Columbus's first voyage, England's king Henry VII granted a patent to John Cabot and his sons, Sebastian, Lewis, and Sancius. (A patent was the necessary authority given by the king to explore a particular region.) In 1497, John Cabot explored the northeastern coast of Canada, from the tip of Newfoundland south to possibly the northern parts of Nova Scotia. Cabot did not find any evidence of a passageway that might lead to the west. Sebastian Cabot claimed to have followed the route of his father in 1508 and went as far north as Hudson Strait; for whatever reason, he went no further north and did not enter Hudson Bay.

In this early part of the 1500s, the most active European explorers were the Spanish and the Portuguese, but they concentrated their search for a route to Asia along the sea route around Africa or in the southern regions of the New World. The Portuguese jealously tried to guard the sea route to Asia around Africa, and the Spanish tried to maintain their authority over the route around the southern tip of South America. Only infrequently did the British or other Europeans challenge the Spanish warships.

AN ALTERNATIVE PASSAGE TO ASIA

For the British and others, an alternative passage needed to be found, if it existed, in the northern regions. Exploration at this point, in the early decades of the 1500s, focused on the entire eastern coast of North America, but the solid landmass of North America seemed impenetrable. Fishermen and travelers, however, continued to bring back accounts of the vast uncharted waterways that lay north of Newfoundland. There were bays, straits, inlets, channels, and sounds, any one of

The Lure of Asia

For many centuries—beginning at least during the time of the ancient Romans—Europeans had considered Asia a source of exotic products and potential wealth. Spices, exotic foodstuffs, and colorfully dyed textiles of silk and wool were sought after by European merchants and sold to royal and genteel customers at exorbitant prices. Expeditions to Cathay—as China was generally known—met along the way with traders from all over Asia and brought back items of gold, silver, ivory, and jade, made into carvings and jewelry of intricate delicacy and beauty. Tapestries and paintings in resplendent colors brought to the European eye fantastical scenes of unfamiliar natural beauty and strange and unimagined peoples. Books, decorated with lavish and colorful engravings, filled with unknown symbols and words, intrigued the European patrons and were further proof of the artistic skill of the artisans of the Eastern world.

For some 2,000 years the main route from Europe to the distant realms of Asia had been overland, along the so-called Silk Road, which was in fact several roads and involved many products in addition to silk. But as the 1400s grew to a close, Muslim peoples—converts to the religion of Islam—had increasingly become a powerful and controlling force in the Middle East. By 1453 most of the Byzantine Empire—the Christian empire with its capital in Constantinople (today Istanbul)—had fallen to Muslim forces, and the overland route from Europe to Asia was extremely hazardous, if not in fact closed. It was this situation that motivated Spain to seek the alternative route to Asia: to the west.

which might lead westward. In 1576 Sir Humphrey Gilbert, an English soldier and an explorer, published a tract called *A Discourse for a Discoverie for a New Passage to Cathaia* in which he attempted to prove that Northwest Passage had to exist to the north. Gilbert concluded that "any man . . . may with small danger passe in Catai [Cathay] . . . and all other places in the East, in much shorter time than either the Spaniard or the Portingale [Portuguese] doth."

This tract was primarily in support of the efforts of his friend Martin Frobisher to undertake a voyage of exploration for the passage in the unexplored regions north and west of Newfoundland. Gilbert's predictions of the vast wealth to be gained through this short route to the Orient excited the interest of London merchants and stirred the deep nationalist feelings already present in Elizabethan society. This was an age where exploration and new discoveries were patriotic endeavors.

Frobisher, a highly experienced seaman, was an explorer, soldier of fortune, and adventurer. Documents of the time accuse him of "fitting out a vessel as a pirate," but this and other legal difficulties were evidently overlooked for he managed to get an audience with Queen Elizabeth, who eagerly approved of his intended search for the passage. Thus it was that England's Muscovy Company, which since 1555 had held the royal patents for English exploration in the New World, was forced to grant permission to Frobisher to pursue his quest.

Frobisher left Blackwall, England, on June 15, 1576, with a party of seamen and three ships. One ship was broken up in a gale and the crew lost. A second ship, damaged by storms and ice, returned to England. But Frobisher pressed on in the *Gabriel*, past the southern tip of Greenland and, although constantly beset by heavy fog, storms, and dangerous drifting ice, reached the southern tip of Baffin Island. Frobisher then entered a bay (later named after him), a wide expansive body of water that he thought was a strait. Observing the mountains on both sides of his "strait," Frobisher concluded that he had found the first part of the passage and that the

Martin Frobisher returned from Baffin Island with fur clothing made by the Inuit; this engraving depicts Inuit of Greenland wearing entire fur outfits. *(National Library of Canada)*

land on the left was America, and that on the right was Asia. Frobisher's conclusion that he had already reached Asia indicates how very little was known about the geography of America and the massiveness and complexity of the northern Canadian archipelago.

After some rather disastrous engagements with the Inuit inhabitants of Baffin Island—five of the Englishmen were captured, never to be seen again—Frobisher returned to England with some furs, an Inuit prisoner (to be put on display), and a quantity of iron pyrite, which the explorers took to be gold ore. So excited were Frobisher's backers over the discovery of what in fact turned out to be fool's gold (pyrite) that they sent him on a second and third voyage to bring back more of the worthless mineral. On Frobisher's third voyage in 1578, he discovered the entrance to Hudson Strait, quite by accident when his ship was blown off course.

After Frobisher's "gold ore" proved conclusively worthless, the search for the passage came back into the focus of London merchants and entrepreneurs. In 1585, a group of businessmen appointed John Davis, a captain recommended by one of his contemporaries as "very well grounded in the principles of the art of navigation," to head another expedition to search for the Northwest Passage. Davis left Dartmouth, England, in summer 1585 and reached the southern tip of Greenland in mid-July. He passed Greenland and proceeded northwest to Baffin Island, passing north of Frobisher's mining excavations, following the eastern shore of Baffin Island. He returned to England and reported to his sponsors that the passage was certain, "nothing doubtful, but at any tyme almost to be passed." He further claimed that the seas were "navigable, void of ice, and the waters very deep."

Because Davis's report was so optimistic, he was sent on a second voyage the following

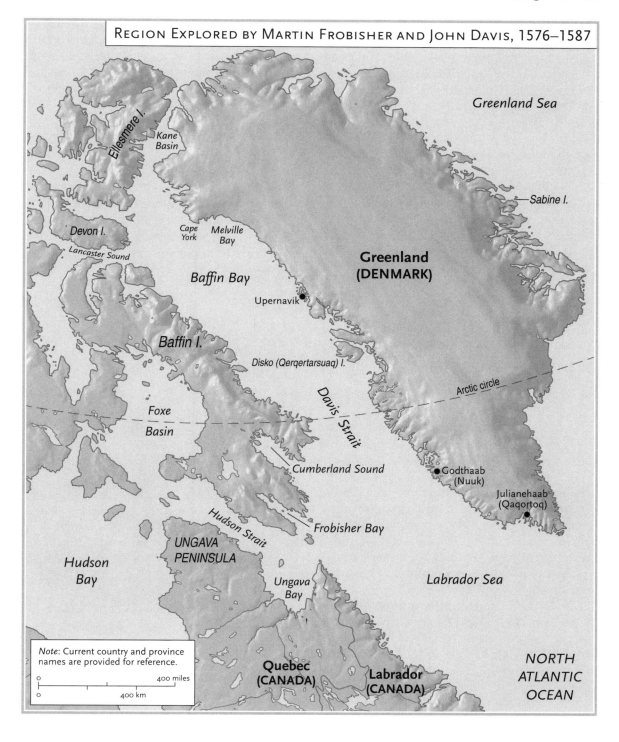

REGION EXPLORED BY MARTIN FROBISHER AND JOHN DAVIS, 1576–1587

Greenland Sea

Ellesmere I.

Kane
Basin

Sabine I.

Devon I.

Cape
York

Melville
Bay

Greenland
(DENMARK)

Lancaster Sound

Baffin Bay

Upernavik

Baffin I.

Disko (Qerqertarsuaq) I.

Davis Strait

Arctic circle

Foxe

Basin

Cumberland Sound

Godthaab
(Nuuk)

Julianehaab
(Qaqortoq)

Hudson Strait

Frobisher Bay

UNGAVA
PENINSULA

Hudson
Bay

Ungava
Bay

Labrador Sea

Note: Current country and province
names are provided for reference.

0   400 miles

0   400 km

Quebec
(CANADA)

Labrador
(CANADA)

NORTH
ATLANTIC
OCEAN

year. The four ships of the party reached Greenland in early summer but found the east coast, as Davis wrote in his logbook, "mightily pestered with yce and snow," so they entered a fjord (narrow inlet) on the west coast for shelter. Davis met the local Inuit and began a friendly exchange of gifts and iron implements for furs, but relations between the Inuit and the explorers deteriorated very quickly, and after some deaths on both sides, Davis retreated to the north, along the western coast of Greenland. There Davis met, for the first time, real arctic weather, even though it was still early fall. Heavy pack ice buffeted the frail ships, and freezing fog coated the mast, rigging, and decks of the ships with black ice (a thin, almost invisible coating of ice). Three of the four ships returned to England. Davis, in the *Moonshine*, went south to the tip of Labrador, where he encountered vast schools of codfish—"the largest and best fed fish I ever sawe," wrote Davis in his logbook—which he set his crew to catching and drying. At the conclusion of a terrible storm, Davis returned to England, reaching home late in 1586.

Davis made a third voyage to North America in 1587, once again getting involved in a series of deadly battles with the now distrustful Inuit. Davis sailed as far north as the weather and ice would permit, 70° N in Baffin Bay, and on his return south, explored Cumberland Sound, proving that it was not the sought-after passage. He had not gone quite far enough north to reach Lancaster Sound, which was the true beginning of the Northwest Passage.

There were several other attempts at the passage in the early 17th century. In 1602 George Waymouth reached 69° N (about midway up Baffin Island), and in 1606 John Knight led an ill-advised and ill-prepared voyage to Labrador that ended in disaster. Determination to find the Northwest Passage began to weaken, but the discoveries of the English explorer Henry Hudson were to provide new optimism and strong motivation for those who never stopped believing that fame and riches would be the eventual rewards of successful exploration.

HENRY HUDSON'S VOYAGES

In 1607 and again in 1608, Hudson had attempted to find a northeast passage to China under the sponsorship of England's Muscovy Company, which still believed that the shortcut might lie across the northern coast of Russia. In 1609, he sailed for the

This painting by John Collier portrays Henry Hudson and his son as they drift in a small boat, presumably to their deaths, with six other crew members after mutineers threw them off the *Discovery*. *(Library of Congress, Prints and Photographs Division [LC-USZ62-128969])*

Henry Hudson explored much of the coast of the United States and Canada in his journeys. This reproduction of a painting by Edward Moran depicts an American Indian family watching Hudson as he explores the coast of what would become New York State. *(Library of Congress, Prints and Photographs Division [LC-USZ62-107822])*

Dutch East India Company on yet another attempt at this route, but when he ran into difficulties, he turned his ship, the *Half Moon,* westward and sailed for North America. There he explored the east coast from Maine to North Carolina, at one point sailing up a river—later named after him—until the grounding of his ship proved that river was not the Northwest Passage. Hudson returned to England in 1609, whereupon he was ordered by King James I to cease his treasonous association with the Dutch. One year later Hudson was commissioned by a group of English merchants to return to North America to explore the regions reported by Davis but never adequately examined.

In 1610 Hudson left England in the *Discovery* with a crew of 20 men. From the beginning, Hudson failed to establish any discipline, and even before the *Discovery* reached Iceland the crew was constantly quarreling. In June 1610, the *Discovery* finally entered Hudson Strait and for a period of time wandered about Ungava Bay, due to bad weather and worse seamanship, and for three weeks the ship was imprisoned by the ice. Finally, the voyagers pressed westward to the end of Hudson Strait and entered the massive inland sea since known as Hudson Bay. Hudson was sure that the western extreme of this bay was China and that he was sailing over the top of North America. He followed the eastern coast of the bay to the south until it began to curve away to the west, after 500 miles of clear easy sailing. This change was a good sign that the passage was heading to Asia.

Fighting the Cold

When the human body begins to chill down, the first parts to suffer are the extremities: the hands, the feet, and the nose. When the body begins to lose heat, the small capillaries near the surface of the skin close, and the blood circulates more deeply for protection to the vital organs. The surface areas begin to freeze, and white patches of frostbite appear on the hands, the toes, and the nose. If not exposed to warmth, the frostbite deepens, and the tissue cells die. As the inner body temperature lowers, physical strength begins to ebb, and thinking becomes cloudy. In the final stages, a sensation of delightful warmth infuses the whole body, and a peaceful sleep comes on from which there is no awaking.

Human beings, like all mammals, are homeothermous, meaning literally "same temperature"; that is, a constant body temperature must be maintained for physical and psychological well-being. But unlike the land and sea animals in the polar regions, humans have neither fur nor feathers and therefore have to use clothing to protect their rather delicate body from the cold.

The chief function of cold weather clothing is insulation. The human body generates heat, but this heat will instantly vanish into the surrounding frigid air unless it is prevented from doing so. The secret of good insulation is to have a layer of air between the body and the clothing, because air is a very good nonconductor of heat. Both fur and feathers trap air within their fibers and reduce the transfer of heat from the body to the outer layers of clothing and thus into the surrounding cold air. Some material is specially adapted by nature to provide maximum insulation.

Suddenly, the shoreline began to tail away to due south. Hudson followed for 200 miles only to find that the shoreline abruptly turned north and the explorers realized that they were in a dead end. They had in fact sailed out of Hudson Bay into James Bay, an appendage of the larger bay. The crew became greatly upset when they realized they had found nothing and winter was approaching. Ice was beginning to form and rations were running out. Hudson then did something odd: He sailed from north to south, east to west, back and forth, seemingly unable to get out of James Bay. He would make a decision, reverse

it when the crew objected, then go off in some other ill-advised direction. Finally, as the ice closed in, the *Discovery* anchored deep in the southwest part of James Bay for the winter. Somehow, despite scurvy (the disease caused by lack of vitamin C) and near starvation, the explorers survived the winter of 1610–11. The dissension continued and intensified, all of this exacerbated by Hudson's erratic and unpredictable decisions.

When the *Discovery* was finally released from the ice, Hudson's decision in June 1611 to continue westward evidently touched off a mutiny. Hudson, his young son, and six loyal

All of the skins used by the indigenous people of the Arctic had their special properties, advantages, and disadvantages. Sealskin, with its tightly packed fine hair, is tough and waterproof; however, it is not warm enough for very cold weather. Polar bear fur provides great warmth and has the virtue of being waterproof, but its great weight and stiffness makes it unsuitable for use when agility is needed. Musk ox fur also is outstandingly warm, but it is also inflexible; in addition, it tends to get caked with blood, grease, and dirt. The eider duck, the arctic hare, and the arctic fox provide useful skins for clothing, but these three skins are too delicate for hard use and require constant maintenance and repair. Caribou skin—with its closely packed, dense hair, and each hair having an air-filled cavity—is by far the best insulating material and has historically been the choice of the Inuit. In preparing the hide, it must first be conditioned by chewing; this was the job of the Inuit women, who were a necessary part of many Arctic expeditions. They also saw to the repair of all clothing (leather is soft against the sharp cutting ice always encountered), and oftentimes sewing had to be done at night.

In the Arctic, clothing must be selected to provide adequate warmth but prevent excessive sweating. Cold weather wear must be kept dry or it loses its insulation properties. The Arctic traveler must juggle the factors of waterproof requirements, heat retention, and sweat prevention and dress accordingly. A wrong choice could mean a frostbitten extremity or worse.

Modern inhabitants and travelers in the polar regions have their choice of many new human-made designs and materials that are lighter and better than the animal skins and furs described above. The earlier explorers, however, had to learn to follow the ways of the indigenous people of the north if they were to survive.

seamen were put in a small boat with a single sack of meal and cast off. They were never seen again. The *Discovery,* with great difficulty, struggled back to England where, for whatever reason, the mutineers were never held to account for their deeds.

NEW EFFORTS BY THE ENGLISH

The voyage of Hudson was tragic and inept, but the discovery of Hudson Strait and Hudson Bay was an optimistic promise (however false) of the existence of a northwest passage.

Robert Bylot, an officer of the *Discovery,* described a great flood tide, coming from the west, in Hudson Bay. This, he and others were certain, was a sure sign that the Pacific Ocean lay on the other side of the bay.

Financial backers such as the Muscovy Company and the newly formed Company of Merchants of London, hoped to find the passage in the region of Hudson Bay. The Hudson tragedy had made maritime authorities aware of the necessity of good organization and sound crews and officers for successful expeditions. The voyage of Thomas Button in 1612 was a model of careful preparation and a

HUDSON BAY AND SITES ASSOCIATED WITH EXPLORERS, 1576–1746

Committee Bay

Melville Peninsula

Fury and Hecla Strait

Baffin Island

Foxe Basin

Repulse Bay

Wager Bay

Frozen Strait

Wager Bay

Foxe Channel

Southampton Island

Salisbury I.

Roes Welcome Strait

Chesterfield Inlet

Nottingham I.

Coates I.

Cape Wolstenholm

Hudson Strait

Eskimo Point

Cary's Swans Nest

Mansel I.

Button Bay

Churchill

Hudson Bay

Churchill R.

Port Nelson

Port Harrison

Nelson R.

York Factory (Prince of Wales Fort)

Belcher Is.

Cape Henrietta Maria

James Bay

Fort George

N

Charlton I.

0   300 miles

0   300 km

sound, experienced crew. Button sailed across Hudson Bay to its western coast; he then explored south along the shoreline, finding no passages west except the Nelson River, which soon proved to be a dead end. Turning north, he then followed the coast as far as he could, ending up at Roes Welcome Sound, in the northwest corner of the bay, just below the Arctic Circle. Button returned to England after a safe and orderly voyage, having established that there were no passages from the central or northern portions of Hudson Bay.

In 1615 an expedition left England under Robert Bylot as captain, with the exceptional navigator and explorer William Baffin as pilot. Baffin had developed his skills in a Spitzbergen whaling fleet; he was unparalleled at navigation and became, in fact, the real head of the expedition. After having discovered the massive Baffin Island to the north of Hudson Strait, Baffin explored carefully the northern part of Hudson Bay. The expedition passed through the Foxe Channel, into the large Foxe Basin, due north of Hudson Bay. Here the party encountered extremely bad weather, dangerous grinding ice floes, and shallow waters. Baffin managed to work his way west to a projection of land in the basin that he named Cape Comfort. Baffin was satisfied that no passage existed in this area and headed home to England.

Baffin made his second voyage in 1616; this time the explorers decided to follow the western coast of Greenland as far as possible. Despite terrible weather and ice-bound water, they reached the extreme northern tip of Baffin Bay, Smith Sound, at 78° N, the farthest north reached by any European up to that time. Baffin turned south and on July 12, 1616, north of Baffin Island, he passed by a broad opening leading west, 40 miles in width. He paused, looked at it, and decided that this passage, like so many others, led nowhere. The channel was Lancaster Sound, the true opening to the Northwest Passage. Baffin's exhaustive explorations had produced nothing except the realization that even if the passage existed, it might be too far north to be practical—or even passable. As Baffin would write in 1616 to one of the sponsors of his voyages:

> Wherefore I cannot but much admire the worke of the Almightie, when I consider how vaine the best and chiefest of hopes of men are in things uncertaine; and to speake of no other than of the hopeful passage to the North-West. How many of the best sort of men have set their whole endeavoures to prove a passage that wayes? . . . Yet, what great summes of money have been spent about that action.

A few more expeditions occurred. Jens Monk, a Dane, undertook a futile and disastrous voyage to Hudson Bay in 1619. English navigators Luke Fox and Thomas James both went on explorations in 1631, examining areas already charted, and proved beyond doubt that the Foxe Basin region held no possibilities. By 1632, the search for the Northwest Passage had virtually come to a halt.

HUDSON'S BAY COMPANY ORGANIZED

Arctic exploration had gone as far as it could for the moment; geographical knowledge and navigational skill would have to advance. Ships would have to be built differently, and better, before the ice-packed waterways of northern Canada could be explored. The enthusiasm of financial backers was gone, in the face of consistently negative results.

There was another major reason why the search for a passage had been temporarily abandoned: The discovery of Hudson Bay had brought to light a treasure trove of potential wealth to be found in America. There were seemingly unlimited supplies of timber, fish and whales, and most important, furs of many kinds. The French had already established posts along the St. Lawrence River and were moving west to the Great Lakes and north toward James Bay. Very quickly, business interests in England sought to enter the very profitable fur trade. In 1670 England's king Charles II granted a charter to the "Governor and Company of Adventurers of England trading into Hudson Bay," the Hudson's Bay Company. The company was granted the rights to all fur trading, all mineral rights, and the power to make peace or war with the native population. Within a few years, there were at least six forts (trading posts) on the western shore of Hudson Bay and south into James Bay. From the beginning, profits to the company were enormous: Stock in the company doubled every two years. Future conflict with the French over the territories and its riches was inevitable, but for the time being, there was enough for all—Europeans, that is: Little or no thought was given to the impact of such activity on the Inuit and other native peoples of North America.

There were a few adventurers not caught up in the lust for the profits from mink, otter, ermine, and especially beaver furs. The dream of a Northwest Passage still existed for James Knight, who managed to get the company to sponsor a search expedition. In 1719, his two-ship party left Gravesend, England, with a promise to return from the East laden with treasures from China. The ships and crew were never seen again; relics were found in 1767 in the northern regions of Hudson Bay.

An English businessman, Arthur Dobbs, was convinced that the passage began off Hudson Bay. Dobbs was so persuasive (and so rich) that he was able to get King George II to sponsor a huge expedition. In June 1741, Captain Christopher Middleton left England and reached Hudson Bay in July. After wintering on the Churchill River, he pressed north and charted thoroughly the northern portions of the bay, including Roes Welcome Sound. He found the waterway that joined Welcome Sound and the Foxe Basin, and dubbed it Frozen Strait, guessing correctly that it was perpetually frozen and impassable. Middleton returned to England, having proven conclusively that there was no exit to the west from Hudson Bay.

Dobbs was unwilling to accept the discouraging truth, and in 1746 he sent William Moor to the same area. Moor verified Middleton's findings. Thus ended any attempt to find a passage from Hudson Bay. The search then continued both by land as well as by sea, and from the west as well as from the east. If a passage did exist, it would have to be discovered on the basis of careful examination of the whole northern boundary of North America and the system of islands and waterways that constituted the Canadian archipelago.

The charter granted to Hudson's Bay Company had specified that the company must continue to search for the Northwest Passage. This mandate had been ignored; the company was too busy making money. In direct response to serious criticism from London merchants and the British Admiralty, the company ordered an expedition to proceed from Prince of Wales Fort, on the western coast of Hudson Bay, to the Coppermine River. The party was to follow that river to the Polar Sea, and if possible find the Northwest Passage. A young naval officer, Samuel Hearne, was put in charge of the mission, and he left the fort in November 1769, heading north and west into territory previously unvisited by Europeans. After several failed attempts, Hearne did indeed find the fabled Coppermine River and followed it to its mouth. He thought he had reached an open Polar Sea and claimed the river and coast on behalf of the Hudson's Bay Company. Hearne's navigation was hugely erroneous; he was hundreds of miles off—both east-west and north-south. Instead, he had reached Coronation Gulf, an inland reach of the Arctic Ocean. Despite his mistaken claims, he had traveled and charted almost 1,000 miles west from Hudson Bay and had proven that no inland waterway or river crossed northern Canada from east to west. His maps were meticulous and were the basis for future exploration of the Canadian northwest.

THE INFLUENCE OF JOHN BARROW

In 1803, a young Englishman named John Barrow was made second secretary to the British Admiralty. Barrow believed passionately in the continued search for the Northwest Passage; during the 40 years of his tenure as secretary he was constant in his support and sponsorship of efforts to discover it. Commercial reward was no longer the main motivation, rather the search, according to Barrow, "had for its primary object that of the advancement of science, for its own sake." In 1818, Barrow backed the expedition of John Ross, who was sent to probe the most northern reaches of the Davis Strait to find a passage to the west. Ross left England in April 1818 and by mid-summer had reached the end of Davis Strait, in Smith Sound, which even at this favorable time of the year was solid ice. Turning south, Ross came to Lancaster Sound, which Baffin before him had identified as a blind bay. Ross sailed 150 miles west into the sound when, suddenly as the mist and fog lifted, he saw before him a group of high icy mountains, blocking further progress completely. Ross returned to England.

Barrow, angered and frustrated at Ross's lack of success, mandated two further explorations: John Franklin was to explore the north coast of North America, east and west of the Coppermine River; William Edward Parry was to repeat the voyage of John Ross and make certain that Lancaster Sound ended at the mountain range, which Ross claimed to have seen. Parry's expedition met with perfect weather and favorable winds. In August 1819 his ships, the *Hecla* and the *Griper,* passed the point where John Ross had seen the "Croker Mountains." What he had seen was an illusion, a common arctic phenomenon based on the refraction of light from broken ice fields.

William Edward Parry discovered the starting point for the Northwest Passage in an expedition that built upon the recent discoveries of John Ross. *(Library of Congress, Prints and Photographs Division [LC-USZ62-100820])*

Ahead lay open water and the explorers sailed easily with a constant easterly wind. In September, after passing and naming numerous islands and inlets, the expedition reached longitude 110° W and thus earned a parliamentary award of 5,000 pounds to be divided among the officers and crew. At longitude 112° W Parry met impenetrable ice, a permanent ice cover that extends from the Beaufort Sea, and was forced to turn back. Parry was given a hero's welcome when the travelers reached London in November 1820. Parry had certainly found the starting point for the Northwest Passage, but he had also found that toward the west the way was blocked by permanent ice. There had to be a point, Barrow reasoned, that the passage dipped south into more hospitable waters.

The mood at the Admiralty by 1823 was optimistic. Franklin had returned from his reconnaissance having charted vast portions of the central part of Canada's north coast east of the Coppermine River. Only a few parts of the Northwest Passage were unknown; the missing parts would be put in place by the next few expeditions. To this end, Barrow authorized four missions in 1824. The first, under Franklin, was to travel to the mouth of the Mackenzie River and explore to the east and to the west along the shore of the Arctic Ocean. The second, under George Francis Lyn, was to proceed overland from northern Hudson Bay to Franklin's Point Turnagain (on the Coronation Gulf, east of the Coppermine River). The third expedition, under Frederick Beechey, was to pass through Bering Strait and explore eastward along what would be the coast of Alaska's border on the Beaufort Sea. Finally, Parry was to enter Lancaster Sound, sail west to the Prince Regent Inlet and follow it south, in order to find a passage from it to the west.

All four expeditions were partially successful, at best; however, one solid achievement was that 1,500 miles of the north coast of Canada became known. The explorations of George Back (1833–34) and Thomas Simpson and Peter Dease (1837–39) completed the charting of the northwest coast of Canada from Point Barrow to longitude 94° W, the point at which the passage had to turn north into the Canadian archipelago. To the east the passage was established; only the central section, perhaps 600 miles, was still in question. John Ross attacked this central region in a four-year expedition (1829–31) but was stopped by ice and frozen in Prince Regent Inlet for three winters. Thus was the setting when in 1845 Franklin set off on his third North American expedition and vanished in the Arctic wilderness.

4

THE SEARCH FOR JOHN FRANKLIN
The Passage Found

There was no word from Sir John Franklin in the summer of 1846. He had been gone just a year; and Franklin himself had said that he expected to be out of touch for at least two years. Besides, everyone in England knew that the *Erebus* and the *Terror* carried enough food to last the expedition for three years. With some hunting and fishing, the supplies could probably be extended to last an additional year. Yet as the end of 1846 grew near, the Admiralty began to feel uneasy.

Sir John Ross wrote a note to the Admiralty in September 1846, reminding those officials that he had made a promise to Franklin to lead a relief expedition in search of him if no word had been received by January 1847. Certainly Ross had grounds for his concern; he himself had been held by the ice for four years in the area Franklin intended to explore. His ship, the *Victoria*, had never broken free and

was eventually abandoned in 1832. Ross asked to be given command of a search mission, but his request was denied.

As 1847 drew to a close, anxiety grew that the Franklin expedition might be in grave danger. The Admiralty assembled a group of senior Arctic explorers, called the Arctic Council, to assist in planning the best and most efficient way to proceed. The difficulty was that no one had the slightest idea where Franklin had gone. And because no contingency plans had been made for the possibility of trouble, there was no prearranged place for Franklin to leave a message.

THE SEARCH FOR FRANKLIN BEGINS

In 1848, the Admiralty, however belatedly, sprung into action. Three separate search parties were organized. The first, under the command of James Clark Ross, nephew of Sir John Ross, was to sail west through Lancaster Sound and look to the north and south for signs of the lost party. The second was to position itself at the far west outlet of the passage, on the faint chance that Franklin had made it through and was stranded somewhere near the Bering Sea. The third search mission was overland. Sir John Richardson, Franklin's companion from two earlier explorations, and John Rae, were to leave Great Slave Lake and travel down the Mackenzie River to the Beaufort Sea. They were then to move east along the coast, in small boats, to the mouth of the Coppermine River.

None of the three search expeditions found any trace whatsoever of John Franklin. The explorers who were waiting near Bering Strait were in a location that Franklin had never come close to reaching. Likewise, Richardson and Ross, on their expedition up the Mackenzie, were hundreds of miles away from Franklin's location.

The search conducted by Ross, although fruitless, was at least in the general region visited by Franklin in the early part of his exploration. Ross managed to get well into Lancaster Sound but could not sail as far west as Franklin had, even though he had arrived at the warmest part of the season. As the weather turned cold in August, Ross found winter shelter on the northeast corner of Somerset Island. In spring, when the deep cold of the arctic winter moderated to a relatively tolerable –20° Fahrenheit Ross conducted a number of sledge parties to the south and to the north. One party traveled 150 miles south down Peel Sound, the route actually taken by Franklin. What Ross saw—unbroken, thick ice, stretching ahead as far as the eye could see—convinced him that no ship could ever have sailed this way through such a permanent barrier. He could not

know, of course, of the exceptional summer of 1846 when the ice had lifted and enticed Franklin into the trap from which he could never escape. The sledge party from the north returned with the same report: All there was was ice. Ross began to fear for his own safe return. In November 1849, he was able to leave his haven at Somerset Island and sail back to England.

Heading one search party for the Franklin expedition, James Clark Ross led the *Enterprise* and *Investigator* in an unsuccessful mission. *(Library of Congress, Prints and Photographs Division [G610.B88 (Case Y)])*

Ross's return to England in November 1849 was a great disappointment to the authorities and the populace. He was criticized for not staying longer and for not finding anything. The Admiralty resolved to find Franklin or solve the mystery of his disappearance in the coming year (1850) by a complete and exhaustive search, with the best officers and the fittest ships. Up to this point, the relief mis-

sions had been the exclusive province of the Royal Navy; from 1850 on, private parties and individuals (with a variety of motives) joined in the search. The frantic search was to produce more knowledge of the Canadian Arctic than had been accumulated during the previous 200 years.

The first search party to leave England in 1850 was commanded by Richard Collinson on the *Enterprise;* second in command was Robert McClure, captain of the *Investigator.* McClure had been lieutenant to James Clark Ross in the Franklin search of 1848–49. The Collinson-McClure party left England early in January 1850: They had to go around South America in order to approach from the Bering Strait. As they were moving into position to begin their search from the western end of the passage, other expeditions were being organized. John Ross, for one, again demanded to be given a mission, and when the Admiralty refused, he privately raised enough money to outfit his own expedition on the *Felix* and prepared to leave for Lancaster Sound.

Lady Jane Franklin, Franklin's wife, sought and received assistance from the president of the United States, Zachary Taylor. With a contribution from businessman Henry Grinnell, along with an appropriation from Congress, the U.S. Navy prepared the *Advance* and the *Rescue* to search the eastern Arctic. Lady Franklin, with her own money and funds raised privately, outfitted the *Prince Albert,* captained by Charles C. Forsyth, to join the numerous expeditions leaving England in the spring of 1850.

Arctic Ice

Arctic explorers traveling above the Arctic Circle would encounter three different types of ice, depending on the following factors: how far north they were; the geographical and meteorological features of the area they were exploring; and the current weather conditions, and possibly the weather conditions of the previous year or two. If the explorers were at the North Pole, they would be on polar ice (also known as the arctic pack), which never melts, although even here there was sometimes open water such as Robert Peary's "big lead." South of the pole and throughout most of the Canadian archipelago the explorers would be in the region of pack ice. At this level, because the pack ice sometimes partially melts in the summer, there is room for the masses and chunks of ice to move, migrate, smash into one another, and form pressure ridges of sheets of ice piled one on top of the other into mountains of impossible debris. Pack ice represents a great challenge to the explorer: Sometimes a ship can sail through it for a while and then suddenly it closes up and the unwary seamen are trapped. It cannot be traversed by sledge without great danger to the traveler: One day the ice is solid and the next day open water bars progress or retreat. Smooth ice can suddenly become filled with pressure ridges 30 feet high that cannot be crossed by sledges. It was pack ice that imprisoned Franklin off King William Island and then hampered his party's attempt to retreat to the south.

The third kind of ice that the explorer would have to deal with, known as fast ice, begins to form at the shore line of any landmass and as it freezes, grows out from the shore to the open water or the waiting pack ice. Fast ice is essentially seasonal; in a normal summer it would not be present in July and August.

The Admiralty sent Collinson and McClure early in 1850 on the long voyage to the western outlet. Later in the year, they sent out a four-ship exploration under the command of Captain Horatio Austin to the eastern entrance. Austin, captain of the *Resolute,* was to search Wellington Channel and Melville Island. Leopold McClintock was aboard the *Assistance;* he was a young officer already highly experienced in Arctic exploration (he had been on James Clark Ross's 1848 search expedition), and on this voyage he was to practice his skills in sledging. Finally, the Admiralty sent out a second two-ship expedition, to back up the Austin flotilla in Lancaster Sound; Commander William Penny, a highly experienced whaling captain, was in charge of the *Lady Franklin* and the *Sophia.*

FIRST EVIDENCE OF FRANKLIN

By summer 1850 there were 12 ships searching for Franklin, most of them centered in the east. At that time there was still no evidence whatsoever of Franklin's route except that he had entered Lancaster Sound. In late summer Lieutenant Edwin J. DeHaven, skipper of the

Because it is new ice every year, it is rarely more than six feet thick, but if the summer thaw does not melt it, the next winter's cover can be very thick. The term *fast* comes from the fact that the ice is attached to the land: It is *landfast*. Anchoring the ice to the shoreline or the beach is a more massive growth of ice called the foot, which does not melt in the summer. In appearance it looks like a tumbled mass of old, irregular ice, with hollows and ridges filled with drifted snow. As the tide beneath it ebbs and flows, it twists and groans with a kind of hinge action that keeps it attached to the new ice sheet. The ice foot often presents a barrier to the explorer who wishes to move onto the land the ice foot is guarding. The Franklin party had to deal with this barrier when they tried to visit King William Island from their frozen-in ships 15 miles offshore.

Seawater, with its salt content, does not freeze like freshwater. The freezing point of salt water is lower than 0° Celsius, and in order to freeze, the salt must be extruded from the water. Thus saltwater ice is salt free; most of the salt migrates downward and increases the salinity of the water below the ice, making it more difficult to freeze. The more ice there is, the colder it has to be for more ice to form. Some of the salt-rich water (brine) makes its way to the surface of the ice, giving it a slick, oily appearance. The new ice is opaque, "tacky" under foot, and elastic, disconcerting to the explorer, who, walking on it, feels that it will give way at any moment.

In the early stages of Arctic exploration, the ice was seen as a scourge and a danger that had to be overcome. Later explorers came to realize that if one knew the movements and the characteristic of the ice, that the ice was the only feasible pathway to the inaccessible regions of the far north; knowing the ice was the key to Arctic travel.

Advance (in the U.S. Navy party) had joined up with the *Assistance* (from the Austin party), and they were searching together. They discovered the first evidence of Franklin's whereabouts: A campsite was found at Cape Riley on Devon Island. Then, on nearby Beechey Island, the searchers found the wintering spot of Franklin's first year in the Arctic; it was marked by cairns and relics, including the grave stones of the first three fatalities of the mission. There was a metal pike in the ground at the beach, with a painted hand sign on it, pointing to the open water. There was no further indication as to where the expedition might have gone.

Lady Jane Franklin funded one of the many search parties sent in pursuit of her husband, Sir John Franklin, and the expedition members accompanying him. *(Library of Congress, Prints and Photographs Division [LC-USZ62-108111])*

Now winter was approaching, and the searchers found the water to the west had closed; passage to Melville Island was no longer possible. The American ships, poorly equipped for winter, turned for home—too late. They became frozen in the lower Wellington Channel and were not freed from the ice until June 1851. Austin and his four ships were frozen in near Cornwallis Island. Captain Forsyth of the *Prince Albert* was able to make his way back to England. The Ross and Penny expeditions found safe harbor and settled in for the winter.

The time spent trapped in the ice was not spent entirely in nonproductive activities; all the explorers took to their sledges and did extensive mapping of uncharted islands and waterways. The most impressive exploration done in the winter of 1850–51 was carried out by McClintock of the *Assistance*. McClintock had studied the techniques used by previous explorations and was aware of the difficulties and problems in the use of a sledge. He knew that the 1,500-pound sledges of the Franklin party would be the death of the men who tried to pull them, so he spent the early winter of 1850 designing, then building new extra-light, strong sledges. Then he devised a method of travel whereby depots of food were left in advance for the traveling party. In April 1851 a large group of men, eager to be on the move after eight months of inactivity, left Cornwallis Island heading south and west. Using McClintock's methods, they traveled and pulled up to 10 miles a day, moving in the night and stopping by day when the slightly warmer temperatures occurred. When there was a favorable wind and smooth ice, sails were installed on the sledges, and they sped forward over the frozen water. Whole new regions were surveyed and charted, such as Wellington Channel, Prince of Wales Island, and Peel Sound. The explorers of Peel Sound reported that the ice

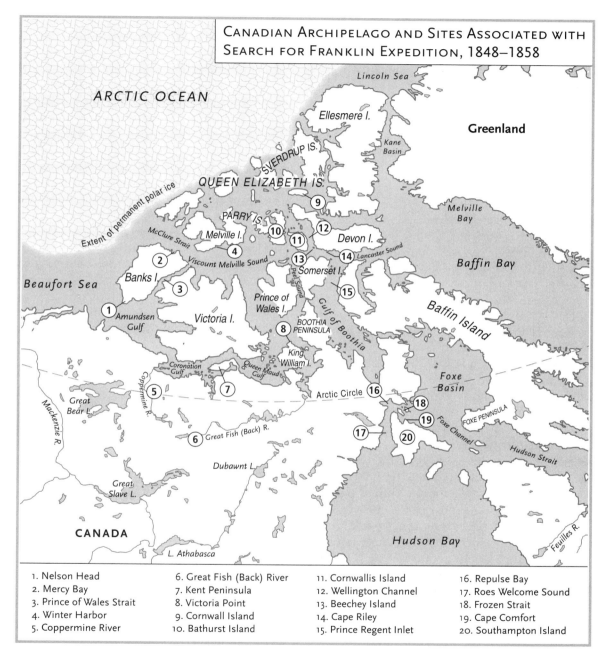

CANADIAN ARCHIPELAGO AND SITES ASSOCIATED WITH
SEARCH FOR FRANKLIN EXPEDITION, 1848–1858

1. Nelson Head	6. Great Fish (Back) River	11. Cornwallis Island	16. Repulse Bay
2. Mercy Bay	7. Kent Peninsula	12. Wellington Channel	17. Roes Welcome Sound
3. Prince of Wales Strait	8. Victoria Point	13. Beechey Island	18. Frozen Strait
4. Winter Harbor	9. Cornwall Island	14. Cape Riley	19. Cape Comfort
5. Coppermine River	10. Bathurst Island	15. Prince Regent Inlet	20. Southampton Island

there appeared to be solid from surface to the bottom. Small wonder that no one believed that Franklin could have gone that way.

McClintock himself went all the way to Melville Island, returning to the *Assistance* in 80 days; he had traveled 770 miles. Altogether the sledging parties had traveled and mapped a total of 7,000 miles. The entire north-central portion of the Northwest Passage was now known and placed on the map. There was, however, no trace of Franklin. The expeditions dispatched to the eastern section of the passage all sailed for home, reaching England in fall 1851.

THE NORTHWEST PASSAGE DISCOVERED

While those parties had been searching in the east, Captain Richard Collinson and Commander Robert McClure had been carrying out their orders by sailing around Cape Horn to reach Alaska from the west. McClure, in the *Investigator,* was to rendezvous with Collinson, the mission commander of the *Enterprise,* off the coast of Alaska. By taking a dangerous shortcut through the Aleutian Islands, McClure got into the Beaufort Sea early and headed straight to the Canadian Arctic coast without waiting for Collinson. The *Investigator* sailed past the mouth of the Mackenzie River, keeping well to the north in the large gulf (later named after Roald Amundsen) that led east along the Canadian coast. McClure found himself in unknown waters; soon he came to and named Nelson Head, at the tip of Banks Island. Just east of that point of land, he entered an undiscovered body of water (Prince of Wales Strait), which angled away to the northeast. McClure had a correct hunch that he was heading toward the western part of the Northwest Passage as seen by Parry in 1819. But before McClure could sail the 60 miles further that would complete the last segment of the passage, the ice closed and the ship was driven back down the strait by wind and moving ice. Sledge parties sent by McClure in the frozen-in winter of 1850–51 verified that they were indeed closing the last link in the Northwest Passage.

The headstrong, ambitious McClure was now determined not to leave the region until he could claim the prize of 10,000 pounds offered for the discovery of the Northwest Passage. When the ice released the *Investigator* in August 1851, McClure tried to sail back down Prince of Wales Strait, up the western coast of Banks Island, and around it to the north. He was almost successful, getting as far as Mercy Bay on the north shore of Banks. There he was frozen in for the winter of 1851–52. In mid-1852 he sent a sledge party to Winter Harbor on Melville Island. There, in Parry's old stone cairn he left a message telling of the starvation and scurvy that was about to bring a fatal end to most of the expedition's members.

Meanwhile, Collinson, arriving at Alaska late in 1850 wisely did not begin exploration until summer 1851. He, too, though unaware of McClure's route, sailed up Prince of Wales Strait and by sledging ascertained that the northern passage existed. He then returned to the Canadian coast and sailed all the way east to Victoria Island. Collinson set out again in 1852 and proved in summer 1853 that there were two branches of the Northwest Passage and that one of them, the northern one, could possibly be traversed by ship.

In England in 1852, the Admiralty was still smarting from the lack of results from its search missions sent out in 1850. They had heard nothing from Collinson and McClure. There was the strong possibility that that search expedition, now long overdue, had met with disaster. Also, there was very little hope that any members of Franklin's party were still alive. After all, it was now seven years since that expedition had set out. Nevertheless, there was strong public pressure to continue the search. Therefore, in April 1852 a major expedition under the command of Edward

Belcher was sent to the Arctic. Belcher was a captain of limited Arctic experience and was reputedly an ineffectual and unpopular leader. A superior had once described his faults to him: "You may be a skillful navigator and a clever seaman, but a great officer you can never be with that narrow mind." However, the presence of experienced Arctic explorers Henry Kellett and Leopold McClintock as captains brought stability and good judgment to the expedition.

Although the mission found out nothing about Franklin, they did manage to find and rescue McClure through the good luck of finding a desperate message from him at Winter Harbor, Melville Island. And because Belcher persistently and erroneously believed that Franklin had gone north of Lancaster Strait, his party discovered new islands and channels as far north as Cornwall Island and mapped and charted hundreds of miles of unknown territory. The "Arctic Squadron," as Belcher's expedition was called, spent the winters of 1852 and 1853 trapped in ice south of Melville Island. In April 1854, Belcher, over the objections of his officers, abandoned four of his five ships, and prepared to return to England in the one able to sail. Then two supply ships arrived and assisted in bringing Belcher's party—including McClure—back to London.

McClure received a hero's welcome, was hailed the discoverer of a Northwest Passage, and was awarded the 10,000-pound prize by Parliament. Belcher returned to a court martial for abandoning his ships but was acquitted.

In no way could the Belcher Arctic Squadron search expedition be called a success, in spite of the useful exploration that had been done. The Admiralty now washed its hands of the whole affair. They had tried; they had spared no expense and had hazarded hundreds of lives in a futile attempt at what was once a rescue attempt but now was merely an attempt to solve a mystery. They were shaken by the near tragedy of the McClure expedition and were determined to risk nothing further. But the lords of the Admiralty were profoundly shaken when the report of John Rae, a Hudson's Bay Company doctor and self-styled solo explorer reached England in 1854.

THE FATE OF THE FRANKLIN EXPEDITION

Rae had begun making solo walks through the Arctic in 1850. He had charted 700 miles of the coastline of Victoria Island on a journey that covered thousands of miles. In 1853, his project was to chart the coastline of Boothia Peninsula while looking for signs of Franklin's expedition. After sailing up the Chesterfield Inlet and finding that he was not going to be able to proceed overland, he turned back and sailed north to Repulse Bay. After wintering there, he set out in March 1854 with four other men, pulling sledges with supplies across the snowy wilderness of Boothia Peninsula.

Heading for the western side of the peninsula, he encountered an Inuit wearing the gilded officer cap of the Royal Navy. Rae let it be known that he would barter for any other such items upon his return. He proceeded west to the Inglis Bay, then turned north to continue his mapping. To his amazement, he discovered a passage of water between Boothia Peninsula and the coast of King William Island, which he named Rae Strait. He had disproved the long-standing myth that King William Land was connected to the mainland. He certainly realized at that moment that the passage to the east of King William Island was the key to the Northwest Passage. The east side was protected from the ice stream and was almost always free of ice year round.

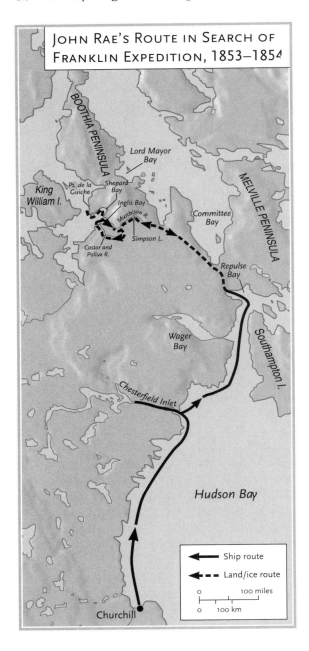

JOHN RAE'S ROUTE IN SEARCH OF FRANKLIN EXPEDITION, 1853–1854

as quickly as possible, Rae turned back. While hurrying back to Repulse Bay, his base, he met a number of Inuit bringing him relics and souvenirs for barter. Included in the items he received was Franklin's Order of Merit and a silver plate engraved with the name *Franklin*. From these Inuit, Rae heard stories of the death marches of the party and of the deaths of the few stragglers who finally reached the mainland. From a trading post on Hudson Bay, John Rae sent a full report of what he had found, including the evidence of cannibalism resorted to by the men in their final desperation for survival. Rae could not have put it more bluntly: "The survivors of the long lost party under Sir John Franklin had met with a fate as melancholy and dreadful as it is possible to imagine."

The mystery was solved; the details of the failed Franklin mission were devoured by a horrified and fascinated public. The Admiralty, aware of its own misjudgments and failure, awarded Rae 10,000 pounds for discovering the fate of Franklin and in effect again closed the book on the affair. Lady Jane Franklin, however, did not. She raised the money for one final voyage. Perhaps there were still, somehow, survivors. Perhaps there were reports, papers, or some clear evidence of what had really happened. And perhaps, most of all, Lady Franklin thought, there might be evidence that the men of her husband's party, albeit on foot, had completed the final link in the Northwest Passage. Lady Franklin was aghast at the suggestion that Rae be the commander of this final search exploration: She was never to forgive his report that suggested the unspeakable practice of cannibalism reported by the Inuit and obviously believed by Rae. She chose instead McClintock, veteran of the previous searches and the clear master of sledge travel.

Realizing that he and his men were in no condition to continue further and deciding it was prudent to get this news back to England

The *Fox*, captained by McClintock, left England on July 1, 1857. It was late summer in 1858 before the *Fox* was able to get into Lancaster Sound. The weather was impossibly bad, and McClintock knew he was not going to benefit from the mild temperature that had allowed Franklin to enter Peel Sound and go south. The party spent another winter frozen in the eastern end of Bellot Strait and then took to the sledges. By April 1859, the party was in position to begin the search on King William Island. McClintock took the east side of the island; Lieutenant William Hobson took the west. From the beginning, the searchers found a multitude of relics: skulls and bones, Royal Navy clothing and buttons, silverware, medals, odd bits of metal and meat tins, all traceable to the Franklin party. Finally, in the summer, Hobson found a cairn at Point Victoria; inside was the report of Lieutenant Graham Gore telling the story of the two years spent by *Erebus* and *Terror* frozen in the ice. Appended to that report was the notice of abandonment of the ship by Crozier and Fitzjames and the intended journey to the mainland, the Back River, and ultimately, an exit. The Inuit supplied the rest of the story, and the relics and skeletons verified the details of the tragedy.

The *Fox* returned to England in 1859 with the revelations that ended the Franklin saga and simultaneously, British involvement in Arctic exploration. By unanimous vote of Parliament, in 1866 a statue of Franklin was erected in London, engraved with the words:

> To the great Arctic navigator and his brave
>   companions
> who sacrificed their lives in completing the
>   discovery of
> the Northwest Passage.
>
> A.D. 1847–8

In search of evidence of the fate of Sir John Franklin's mission, Lady Jane Franklin, his wife, funded a voyage by Leopold McClintock, who discovered many belongings that were definitively linked to the Franklin party. These skulls were found by later explorers. *(National Archives of Canada)*

AMUNDSEN NAVIGATES THE NORTHWEST PASSAGE

British explorers had striven many years in their search of a northwest passage, and it had ended in the dark tragedy of the Franklin party. But what had happened to the *Erebus* and *Terror* could never overshadow the incredible achievements of the many years of explorations. Roald Amundsen, the first man to sail through the passage, certainly recognized that his success was based on the efforts and sacrifices of the great men who had come before.

Amundsen had been a student of the Arctic since his boyhood when he slept with his window open to the Norwegian winter to acclimate himself to the cold. As a young man he read about the Franklin tragedy, and

he was familiar with the other great Arctic explorers. Amundsen later wrote, "I, too, would suffer in a cause." After studying medicine for a while, Amundsen quit medical school to join the navy; after an Antarctic expedition, he returned to Oslo where he bought (on credit) a ship, the 72-foot, 47-ton *Gjöa* into which he installed a 13-horsepower diesel engine, and with borrowed money, stocked it with five years' worth of provisions. He assembled a crew of six: Godfred Hansen, Anton Lund, Peder Restvedt, Helmer Hansel, Gustav Wük, and Adolf Lindstrom.

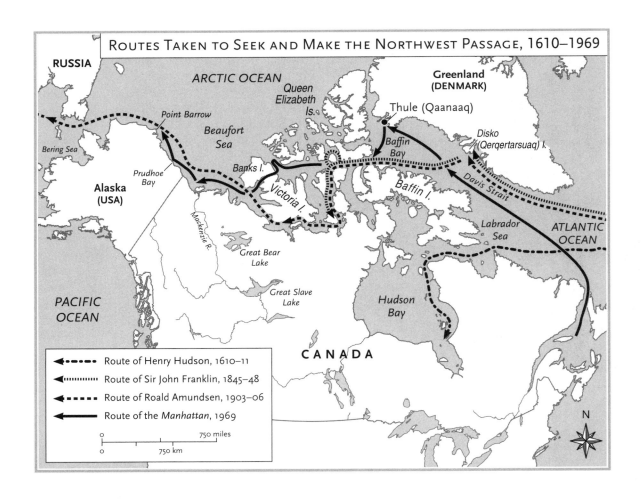

ROUTES TAKEN TO SEEK AND MAKE THE NORTHWEST PASSAGE, 1610–1969

◄•–•–• Route of Henry Hudson, 1610–11

◄•••••••• Route of Sir John Franklin, 1845–48

◄•–•–• Route of Roald Amundsen, 1903–06

◄■■■ Route of the *Manhattan*, 1969

750 miles

750 km

Shown here is the deck of Roald Amundsen's *Gjöa* in 1906 after Amundsen had become the first person to lead an expedition all the way through the Northwest Passage. *(Library of Congress, Prints and Photographs Division [LC-USZ62-122067])*

(Andreas Pedersen is listed as a member of Amundsen's crew but did not accompany him on this journey.) Under cover of darkness (to avoid arrest for debt), Amundsen and crew slipped out of Oslo harbor, headed for the fulfillment of one of his dreams, the navigation of the Northwest Passage. Amundsen left Norway on June 16, 1903, and made his way to Gjøa Haven on the southeastern coast of King William Island on September 9, 1903, where he remained locked in

the ice for two years. He put his waiting time to good use by carrying out numerous scientific observations and relocating the North Magnetic Pole. Amundsen was a skilled winter traveler and had brought dogs on the *Gjöa* for his sledging. He made extensive sledge journeys and spent a great deal of time with the Inuit, learning all he could from them about the Arctic.

On August 13, 1905, the ice suddenly opened. The *Gjöa* sailed around King William

Some Conquests of the Northwest Passage after Roald Amundsen

The first ship to navigate the Northwest Passage after Roald Amundsen's historic voyage in 1903–06 was the *St. Roch,* a vessel of the Royal Canadian Mounted Police (RCMP). The commander of the expedition was Henry A. Larsen, a Canadian corporal in the RCMP; the purpose of the voyage was to demonstrate Canadian sovereignty of the Arctic to the international community, as during the first half of the 20th century, exploration and activity in the Arctic were being taken over by Canadians and Americans. Larsen left Vancouver in June 1940 with the intention of traversing the passage from west to east; the RCMP base at Halifax, Nova Scotia, was to be the destination. Larsen hoped to reach Gjöa Haven (on King William Island) before winter set in, but instead the *St. Roch* was frozen in not only for the first winter, but the second winter as well. The *St. Roch* reached Halifax in 1942 and then, after installing a larger engine, returned to Vancouver via the northern branch of the Northwest Passage.

The *Gjöa* and the *St. Roch* were both small ships, built to tiptoe carefully through shallow water and ice-filled channels. The next ship to navigate the passage was not built for maneuverability or speed but for brute strength. The HMCS *Labrador* was a deep-draft Canadian navy icebreaker, designed to force its way through ice of any thickness. It was 250 feet long, weighed 6,000 tons, and had a top speed of 16 knots. In 1954, the *Labrador* pounded its way through the ice of the northern passage in 68 days (compared to the *St. Roch*'s voyage of 28 months). The *Labrador* was never seriously challenged by the ice because

Island and into Queen Maud Gulf. Then the *Gjöa* navigated the shallow waters of Dease Strait and into Coronation Gulf—charted territory at last! Finally on August 27, 1905, just as Amundsen was falling asleep after a watch, he was awakened by a shout: "Vessel in sight, sir." An American whaler was approaching—from the west! "Victory was ours!" wrote Amundsen in his journal. Ahead lay the Beaufort Sea, Bering Strait, and Asia.

There are things that human beings do —individually and cooperatively—that defy explanation. The 350-year quest for a Northwest Passage is one of these things. It is understandable that powerful and ambitious entrepreneurs should seek to reap the incredible wealth that a short passage to China would provide. Such motives are clear. But why would generations of seamen—thousands of officers and crew—will-of the power and reliability of its diesel engines. In addition, it had large water tanks on both sides that when filled and emptied caused a rocking motion that could free it from the tight grip of the ice. The *Labrador* carried two helicopters on deck for emergency use.

In 1957, the *Labrador* was joined by a U.S. icebreaker and two tender ships and sailed through the passage again, this time going by way of Bellot Strait. In so doing, it established a new route for deep-draft ships and shortened the journey by hundreds of miles.

In the 1960s, a group of oil companies set out to determine whether it was feasible to ship oil from Alaska to the east coast of the United States. To this end, the group financed the design and construction of a massive super-tanker that could steam freely through the northern Northwest Passage. The *Manhattan* was specially designed; Like Fridtjof Nansen's *Fram,* it had a rounded bow that rode up over the ice and allowed the weight of the ship to come down on the ice and shatter it. The *Manhattan* weighed an incredible 150,000 tons and was driven by a diesel unit that produced 43,000 horsepower (compared to the *St. Roch*'s 150 horsepower engine). In 1969, the *Manhattan,* accompanied by two U.S. icebreakers, made the trip from east to west in record time, leaving Pennsylvania on August 24 and arriving at Point Barrow, Alaska, on September 1. On the return trip, however, the ship was severely damaged by the ice. It was concluded that the use of the passage for the transportation of oil was not practical. It seems unlikely that further attempts will be made to use the passage for commercial purposes.

ingly submit themselves to the proven agony of Arctic exploration? Somehow, in the struggle and travail of exploration, some basic, essential virtue of humankind comes to the fore, overwhelming and making insignificant such a motive as profit-making. The passion that these early explorers brought to their quest was unquenchable; collectively, the force of their determination was irresistible.

And so, after all the years, the Northwest Passage was conquered. It was of no consequence that there was no commercial value to this victory; that illusion had been lost years before. What was important was that the perseverance, heroism, and suffering of the countless explorers before seemed now to be justified. New challenges lay ahead, and they would be faced with equal determination and passion.

5

APPROACHES FROM THE EAST

 The British had initiated the search for a Northwest Passage as a way of reaching the treasures of Asia. The hoped-for route lay atop North America and would avoid the long voyage around the tip of South America. Aside from the harsh climate and seas, these southern waters were controlled by the Spanish, who fiercely resisted the efforts of any other nation to pass through them. Eventually, the Northwest Passage was found, but it proved to be of little use as a trade route: Most of it was too frozen to be traversed by ordinary ships. But long before the dream of a Northwest Passage faded, there were those who believed that a better, faster pathway to the East existed: the Northeast Passage.

The Northeast Passage would begin at the northern tip of the Scandinavian Peninsula and proceed eastward along the coast of Europe and Asia to the Bering Strait and thus to the northern Pacific Ocean. From there would be a short run south to Japan and China. Given the belief in the 16th century that the Earth was much smaller than it actually was, geographers had no idea how far it was from Norway to the Bering Strait, or from there to Japan. In fact, the existence of a strait between the Arctic Ocean and the Pacific was not even certain. The difficulty was that gentlemen merchants in London and Amsterdam theorizing about this Northeast Passage (and actually loading up and sending off trading ships) had no sense whatsoever about the northeastern part of Russia: how far north it extended, what kind of seas bordered it, and what kind of people, if any, inhabited it. Even the Russians did not know what lay to the farthest east and north.

EARLY ENGLISH EFFORTS

It was with a great deal of baseless optimism that a group of merchants in London, eager for profits, formed a private company in 1553 with the modest title of "Company of the Merchant Adventurers of England for the discovery of lands, territories, isles, dominions and regnoires unknown." This company was incorporated in 1555 and became known as the Muscovy Company. The organization was interested in the northwest or northeast or any route that led to the riches of the Far Eastern civilizations. One of the governors of the Muscovy Company was Sebastian Cabot, who with his father, John, had sought the Northwest Passage. Cabot believed strongly in the existence of a route to the northeast. He relied first on the story in King Alfred's *Chronicles* of the ninth-century voyage of the Viking Othere from Norway to the White Sea in Russia (the White Sea lies due north of Moscow). Furthermore, a contemporary of Cabot, a merchant named Gre-

gory Istoma, described a voyage he had taken from the White Sea to Trondheim (northern Norway) in the company of a number of ships on a trading mission. Cabot also noted that there were rumors of established trade between Russian cities and ports on the Scandinavian Peninsula. Cabot reasoned that if voyages to the

Siberia and the Northeast Passage

The Northeast Passage, the sea route that runs 5,000 miles along the Arctic coast of Russia and Siberia, begins at Murmansk, Russia, and ends at the Bering Strait. At Murmansk the latitude is 70° N, four degrees above the Arctic Circle; Cape Dezhneva, at the beginning of the Bering Strait is approximately at the Arctic Circle. In order to sail from one to the other, it is necessary to go far above 70° N because the Siberian coastline projects up toward the North Pole with vast headlands, protruding capes, and archipelagos. The Kola, Kanin, and Yamal Peninsulas were obstacles for early explorers, who had to keep close to the coast to avoid the polar ice. Novaya Zemlya, a pair of islands, caused explorers major difficulty, and the attempt to go north of them was the undoing of a number of missions. But the most insuperable barrier was the Taimyr Peninsula, which stretches from the mainland to 76° N, the northernmost extension of the Eurasian mainland. The Russians who participated in the Great Northern Expedition (1738–41), charged with mapping the Arctic Siberian coastline, found it impossible to sail around it and instead explored it on land. Not only was there the regular winter (10 months) ice to contend with; there were ice clusters, unpredictable masses of ice that formed and dissipated without warning (there are nine of these pockets of ice from Murmansk to Cape Dezhneva). If a ship managed to get around the tip of the Taimyr Peninsula, the Laptev Sea was waiting. Of all the seas that lie between the Arctic Ocean and the mainland (Barents, Kara Laptev, East Siberian, and Chukchi), the Laptev is the stormiest and the most icefilled.

Emptying into the various seas along this vast waterfront are a number of rivers, the major ones being the Pechora, Ob, Taz, Yenisei, Lena, Kolyma, and the Anadyr. All of these rivers run from deep in the interior of Siberia. The few indigenous people who lived there in the early days tended to be clustered around the rivers, particularly at the mouths, where there was at least some communication with people from the more developed and populated regions to the west. These inhabitants traded with one another, although the peninsulas

(continues)

(continued)

formed barriers that severely limited contact. The network of rivers was a positive factor in the development of the Siberian north: They were routes by which the indigenous inhabitants could bring their products for trade to the small villages that eventually began to form along the coast. At first the products were mainly furs; eventually lumber, reindeer meat, and hides were bartered. In more modern times, valuable ores—tin, lead, zinc, copper, and gold—came down the rivers to the picked up by ships venturing along the coast from the west.

The Siberia Arctic, from the earliest days of exploration, was a more viable region than the Canadian Arctic. There were always many more inhabitants; because of overland routes, travel was always easier. What was once a wasteland is in modern times an area of promise and potential economic riches. The Northeast Passage has been largely responsible for the transformation.

White Sea area were possible, then it could not be that much farther to the Pacific.

Consequently, the Muscovy Company had three ships constructed for a voyage along the Arctic coast of Russia to the end of the continent and south into the Pacific and thence to China. The ships, the *Bona Esperanza,* the *Bona Confidentia,* and the *Edward Bonaventure* (named for Edward VI, England's reigning teenage king) were solidly constructed of seasoned oak and sheeted with lead for protection against the worms that would inhabit the warm waters to be eventually encountered. Sir Hugh Willoughby was appointed to command, and Richard Chancellor was pilot major and second in rank. The party left London in May 1553 and included 11 members of the Muscovy Company. Sebastian Cabot, being in his 70s at the time, remained in London.

The explorers sailed north around the tip of Norway (North Cape) and were to rendezvous soon after at Vardø, a port on an islet off the extreme northeastern coast of Norway. However, bad weather scattered the three ships, and Willoughby, who was very inexperi-

enced in all aspects of seamanship, drifted off course to the north with two ships reaching about 72° N. Turning east at this point, he ran into an unknown island, Novaya Zemlya, which he took to be the mainland of Russia. Compounding his errors, he headed off to the north where he soon encountered heavy storms and dangerous ice. Willoughby eventually retreated to the Kola Peninsula (western Russia) where he sought a wintering place. It is known that the ships reached land in an uninhabited area, and all members of the two ships died over the winter. Willoughby's journal (found later) gave no clue to explain the tragic conclusion; it is assumed that cold, exposure, inexperience, and despair brought an end to the ill-advised adventure.

Meanwhile, Chancellor, having waited a week at the rendezvous, sailed to the east and reached the Divina River, which empties into the White Sea, and there encountered friendly and curious inhabitants. Eventually, Chancellor abandoned his search for a sea passage and traveled overland by sledge to Moscow, to the court of Ivan the Terrible, where he was royally treated. When he returned to England, he brought with him papers and agreements that were the basis of a substantial Anglo-Russian trading relationship that was carried on for many years.

The Muscovy Company was impressed with Chancellor's account of the splendor of Ivan's court. They convinced themselves that China must be very close to the White Sea, probably just past the massive island (Novaya Zemlya) that was blocking the way to the east. (They were wrong by about 4,000 miles.) Therefore, a mission was organized under the command of Stephen Burrough in 1556, to sail

east and to get past Novaya Zemlya into what was known as the Kara Sea. Despite the help of some Russian seamen Burrough encountered near Murmansk, he was unable to get past Novaya Zemlya because of its rough seas and what his journal referred to as "monstrous whales." An attempt by another English seaman, James Bassedine, in 1568 got no further.

At this point, the Muscovy Company turned its attention to a Northwest Passage, putting its support behind the exploits of Martin Frobisher. An officer of a Frobisher expedition, Charles Jackman, persuaded the company to sponsor one more search voyage

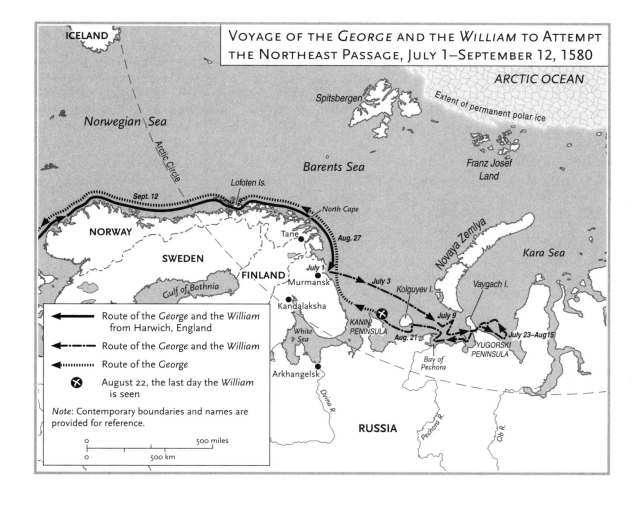

VOYAGE OF THE *GEORGE* AND THE *WILLIAM* TO ATTEMPT THE NORTHEAST PASSAGE, JULY 1–SEPTEMBER 12, 1580

Route of the *George* and the *William* from Harwich, England

Route of the *George* and the *William*

Route of the *George*

August 22, the last day the *William* is seen

Note: Contemporary boundaries and names are provided for reference.

to the East. Jackman was given command of the *William,* while his friend Arthur Pet (who had sailed with Richard Chancellor) was given the *George,* and so confident was the Muscovy Company of their success that they were commissioned, when they arrived among the people of China to "shewe them one of the Queenes Majesties [Elizabeth I] letters, which she sendeth with you . . . written in Latin." The ships left England on May 30, 1580, and sailed around North Cape, headed for the narrow strait between Novaya Zemlya and mainland Russia. With good seamanship and some luck, they passed into the Kara Sea; they were probably the first to visit these waters, other than Russian hunters and fishers. They made little progress in the Kara Sea. Winter was approaching and the ice was already thick and impassable; between July 23 and August 15, they were effectively trapped in ice. The ships turned back on August 16, and on August 22, Pet's journal of the voyage recorded, "with a great fogge we lost sight of [the *William*] and since we have not seene her." Pet's ship made it back to England by December 25; Jackman's ship wintered at a port along the northern coast of Norway, but after setting out again in February 1581, the ship with all aboard was lost. Pet told of his discovery to interested merchants in London and his ship's journal was published. For the most part, it was a routine mariner's log, recording the depth soundings, directions sailed, weather conditions, fog, and ice, with only the occasional expression of feelings, such as "God be thanked the storme began to slacke, otherwise we had beene in ill case." Translated into Dutch, it was read eagerly by businessmen and explorers in Holland.

THE DUTCH EFFORTS

A Dutchman, Oliver Brunel, had for years resided in Russia, in the White Sea area, as a trading agent for some Dutch merchants. As such, he came to speak Russian and to hear of the activity and journeys of many Russian travelers. Brunel had heard that Russian ships regularly made trips from the White Sea to the Ob River and then on further east to the Yenisei River (about 80° E) where there was good wintering. The Yenisei runs into the Kara Sea near the western edge of Siberia; what lay beyond the Yenisei was only to be guessed, as very little was known in the late 16th century about Siberia and its Arctic coast. Russian Cossacks, the semi-independent armies that dominated the frontiers of Russia, had only just begun to claim Siberia and to move eastward across the vast frozen wastelands that were the northern reaches of Siberia. But the Russian travelers encountered by Brunel maintained that there was open water beyond the Yenisei River, and Brunel was certain that the Pacific was not far from that open water. He would have been discouraged had he known the truth: East of the Yenisei lay 3,000 miles of brutal Arctic coastline before the Bering Strait gave access to the Pacific Ocean.

It was, then, with misguided confidence that Brunel in 1584 loaded a ship with trading goods and headed east. He turned back before reaching the Kara Sea and smashed his boat to pieces halfway back to the White Sea. The Dutch were nonetheless determined to find a northeast passage. In 1594, an ambitious expedition was organized under the command of William Barents on the *Mercurius,* seconded by Brandt Tetgales and Cornelius Nay. Tetgales and Nay were to go to the south of Vaygach Island and east into the Kara Sea; Barents was to sail around the northern part of Novaya Zemlya and into the northern Kara Sea. They were then to go as far east as possible, but Barents could not get around the northern tip of Novaya Zemlya: There was too much ice. He returned to the mainland of Russia and learned that Tetgales and Nay had sailed into the Kara Sea but had been blocked by ice almost immediately.

Barents still believed that the passage would lie north of the massive island of Novaya Zemlya, which seemed to block all ships' passage from west to east. When he was made head of an expedition sponsored by Dutch merchants, he and Jan Cornelius Rijp sailed from Holland in 1597; they soon parted company because Barents insisted on attempting again to go north of the island. Once again the ice stopped progress to the east or north; suddenly, retreat was cut off and the ship was crushed in the ice just off shore of Novaya Zemlya. The crew carried stores and tools from the ship to prepare for the 10 months of winter siege by building a huge house on shore.

Early in November the Sun sank out of sight, not to be seen for three months, as the bitter arctic cold set in, unlike any experienced by these explorers. Barents's journal records a typical day: "December 12: extreme cold, so that the walls inside our house and our bunks were frozen a finger thick with ice; yea, and the very clothes upon our backs were white all over with frost and icicles." Incredibly, the entire party survived the winter of 1596–97, although spring found them weak and suffering from scurvy. In June, as the ice began to break up, the 14 men loaded up the small ships' boats and began the 1,000-mile journey to the mainland. It was a horrific ordeal. Barents wrote in his journal: "Every minute of every hour we saw death before our eyes." Three men died before they finally reached the Kola Peninsula and by luck encountered Jan Rijp, who was looking for them. Barents did not survive the journey home, and his body was lowered into the sea that now bears his name. For the next 282 years only snow, wind, and polar bears visited the house he had built until a Norwegian fishing boat crew found the collapsed refuge with

pots, pans, books, and guns still in place in 1879. Among the debris was a chest full of religious prints intended to convert the "heathen" Chinese to Christianity.

After 1600, belief in the Northeast Passage began to wane. The Muscovy Company was prepared, however, to make one last attempt. In 1607 and again in 1608, Henry Hudson sailed around North Cape and then northeast and brought back some useful information about Spitsbergen and Novaya Zemlya; he also probably showed that it was pointless to go north, toward the Pole, as a way of getting to the East. But he did not make any progress whatsoever along the Russian Arctic coast. Then in 1609, Hudson was hired by the Dutch to sail east by first going *north* of the troublesome Novaya Zemlya island, then back south to the mainland and east to the end of Russia. He was not to be paid if he did not follow the explicit orders. This stipulation must have been added because Hudson had made it clear he did not really believe in an eastern passage. Hudson sailed from Amsterdam in his ship, the *Half Moon,* and after rounding North Cape and heading north to Novaya Zemlya, the *Half Moon* encountered impossible weather and heavy ice, and his motley crew refused to go further. Hudson retreated, eventually to pursue his significant exploration in search of the Northwest Passage and his discovery of Hudson Bay. As threatened, the Dutch did not pay Hudson, nor is there any evidence that he pressed a claim.

THE RUSSIANS LOOK EASTWARD

Although by the early 1600s the English and the Dutch were losing interest in a northeast passage, by the late 1500s Cossacks—the military units of self-governing communities in Russia—were pressing further and further eastward in order to establish domination

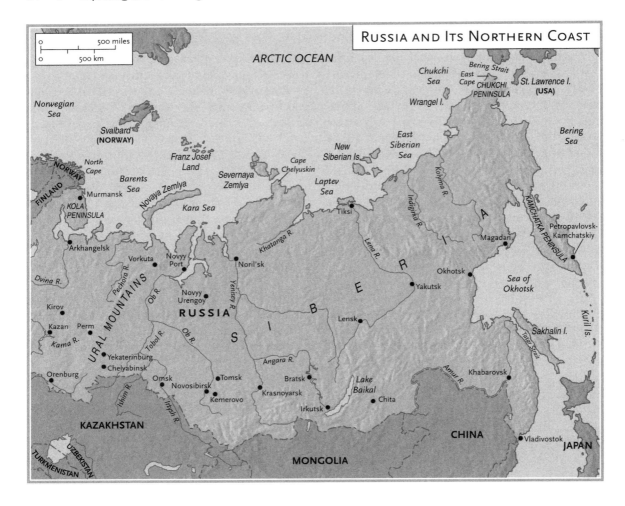

RUSSIA AND ITS NORTHERN COAST

over the vast, unknown territories. A number of trading posts and settlements had been established along the Arctic coast of Siberia, but it would be the end of the 17th century before the Cossacks had reached and settled the Pacific coast of Siberia. There were native groups in northern Siberia who were as determined as the Cossacks: In particular, the Koryaks and the Chukchi fought fiercely to resist the Cossack intrusion into what they considered to be their land. In the meantime, trading went on among the native inhabitants of the 5,000 miles of Artic coastline as it always

had, and bundles of beautiful furs continued to arrive in St. Petersburg: sable, otter, arctic fox, and seal. It was inevitable that some enlightened Russian ruler would decide to systematically explore and put on the map the dimensions and the potential of the vast unknown region.

Czar Peter the Great (1672–1725) was the enlightened ruler of Russia who laid the foundation for Russia's sustained exploration of its extensive northern territories. Peter was concerned with empire and expansion, but he was also interested in geography and knowledge in general. In 1719, he sponsored an expedition to Kamchatka Peninsula (of the northeastern coast of Siberia) to find out if Asia and America were joined by a land bridge, still an uncertainty at this time. The expedition was not successful, but Peter soon organized another mission, carefully planned and headed by the best naval officer available. Vitus Bering, a Danish officer who had spent 20 years in the Russian Naval Service, was chosen to command. Bering was highly experienced in arctic service and was a master of navigation; he was also a man of great fortitude and integrity, though somewhat overcautious and conservative in decision making. Bering's orders were clear but demanding. He was to proceed to Kamchatka and build a boat. Then he was to sail north along the coast of Siberia and see if it joined the coast of America. He was to contact settlements along the way (as well as any ships encountered) and get information wherever he could. Then he was to make charts of everything encountered and return them to St. Petersburg. Everything he needed by way of supplies or materials for ship building (except for wood) he was to carry with him. Never mind that Kamchatka was 5,000 miles away, over mountains and bogs and rivers and across Arctic tundra, and that once in Siberia what few habitations he came across were likely to be hostile.

Bering left St. Petersburg in 1724; part of the journey was made by water along the northern coast but soon the frozen Arctic waters forced Bering inland. It was June 1726 before Bering reached the village of Yakutsk, deep in interior Siberia, a desolate spot surrounded variously by high mountains and endless swamps. Due to the extreme cold and starvation, the final overland push to Okhotsk, on the east coast of Siberia, took a toll of bag-

Vitus Bering for whom the Bering Strait is named lived in this house. *(Library of Congress, Prints and Photographs Division [LC-DIG-prok-02381])*

gage horses and men. Bering built a boat at Okhotsk and sailed it to Kamchatka Peninsula, but Bering was afraid to sail around the peninsula, so the party crossed it on foot and built another ship, the *St. Gabriel.* Four years after leaving St. Petersburg, Bering was ready to set sail.

Bering visited and named St. Lawrence Island (now part of the United States) and sailed north through a strait, thus proving that Asia and North America were separate landmasses, but he did not *see* the strait because of heavy fog. Had it been clear at the right time, he might have seen Asia on his left and North America on his right. On his return to St.

Petersburg, Bering's government sponsors were annoyed that he had not brought back more conclusive evidence (of the strait that was eventually named after him), but he was soon back in the court's good graces. On the basis of Bering's voyage, the St. Petersburg Academy of Sciences published an erroneous map that showed Alaska to be an island, with a passable strait running to the east of the landmass and extending all the way to the Polar Sea.

In 1732, Bering was made administrator of the Great Northern Expedition, which had as its goal the mapping of the entire Arctic coastline of Siberia. This major project continued

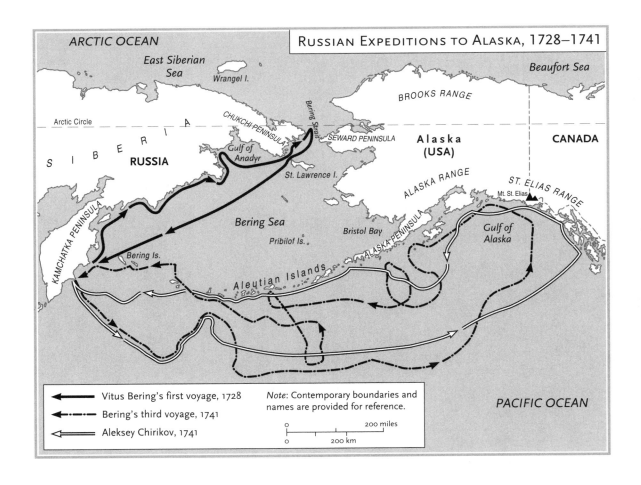

This historical map shows one cartographer's interpretation of Russian discoveries, among them those of Vitus Bering. *(Library of Congress)*

for 10 years and was largely successful. Bering himself did not participate in this mapping but instead set out in 1733 with another expedition to the Kamchatka Peninsula, from which base he proposed to sail to North America. It was June 1741 before he was able to sail forth in the *St. Peter,* accompanied by the *St. Paul* under the command of Aleksey Chirikov. The two ships soon became separated, and Bering's ship sailed all the way to the southern coast of Alaska, where in July some of his party briefly landed on an offshore island. Bering's party also sighted Mount St. Elias, the fourth highest peak in North America. (That same month some of Chirikov's crew landed on one of the Aleutian Islands

before returning to Siberia in October.) On his way back to Kamchatka, Bering's ship ran into foul weather, and one by one his crew became ill and died; by November the survivors had reached an island off the Kamchatka Peninsula where Bering died (and which now bears his name). Bering would forever be honored as the first European to prove that Asia and North America were not linked by land yet that the latter could be reached relatively quickly by sea.

It should be noted, however, that some of Bering's discoveries may have been anticipated by the explorations of Simon Dezhnev and Feodor Popov in 1648. They are reputed to have traveled from the Kolyma River in northeastern Siberia, eastward across the East Siberian Sea and around the Chukchi Peninsula, and then down into the Bering Sea. This voyage would have both discovered the Bering Strait and proved that Russia and North America were not linked, but records of Dezhnev's voyage were not found until the 18th century, and his achievements are still disputed by most historians. In any case, it was Bering's expeditions and his work with the Great

The Russians and North America

Although little known to non-Russians, Russia's ventures into North America did not end with Vitus Bering's expedition. And even though not all of Russia's claims of discovery are accepted by other nations, there is no denying that for an entire century Russians were active along the coast and interior of Alaska. The Russians claim, for example, that on a 1732 voyage Michael Gvosdev and Ivan Federov were the first to sight the easternmost promontory of Alaska, that came to be known as the Seward Peninsula. During the next 37 years, the Russians also credit a number of their compatriots with exploring the coast of Alaska and discovering almost all of the Aleutian Islands. None of these Russians, however, appears to have ventured very far into mainland Alaska.

By 1784, however, a Russian fur trader, Gregory Shelikof, was establishing a trading post on Kodiak Island, just off the Alaska Peninsula, the first non-native settlement in Alaska. In the decades that followed, countless Russians came to Alaska, both to advance the Russian fur trade and to explore the coast and points inland. In the early 1790s, Aleksandr Baranov sailed on several expeditions that explored the coast of Alaska; his activities led to his appointment (1799–1818) as the first manager of the newly founded Russian-American Company, which took the lead in Russia's fur trade, settlements, Christian missions, and exploration in North America.

In the 1790s, Vasily Ivanov may well have traveled all the way to the Kuskokwim and Yukon Rivers; if so, he was the first European to explore the interior of Alaska. Otto von Kotzebue, a Russian of German descent, served on the first Russian ship to make a round-the-world voyage (1803–06); between 1815 and 1818, Kotzebue led an expedition that sailed up through the Bering Strait and discovered the sound along the west coast of Alaska that he named after himself. In 1819–22, Mikhail Vasil'ev, a Russian naval officer, commanded a Russian round-the-world expedition charged with finding a passage from the northern Pacific westward to the northern Atlantic. After eventually sailing north through the Bering Strait, he spent two years trying to find a route through the Arctic Ocean but failed to do so. Between 1825 and 1839, Mikhail Teben'kov commanded surveys of the waters along Alaska's coast. In 1829 and 1830, Ivan Vasil'ev, traveling on foot or in small boats, went into the interior of Alaska and explored the drainage region of the Kuskokwim and Yukon Rivers. In 1834, Andrei Glazunov—son of an Aleut mother and Russian father—went into the Alaskan interior to explore along the Yukon River with the goal of establishing a

Northern Expedition that were influential in the charting of the entire eastern passage and route to the Far East. It now remained for some future seaman to navigate the Northeast Passage.

THE NORTHEAST PASSAGE ACHIEVED

It was many years after Bering's discoveries that exploration of the Northeast Passage

trading post there. And in 1838, Alexander Kashevarov, also son of an Aleut mother and Russian father, led an expedition that explored the coast of Alaska from Kotzebue Sound to Point Barrow. As pioneering and worthy as these Russian explorers, expeditions, and findings were, most went completely unrecognized by people outside Russia and Alaska, and they have received little notice in most histories of exploration in North America.

Russian explorers established settlements and spread Christianity throughout the parts of North America they explored. This Russian chapel at Fort Ross was built in the early 19th century in Sonoma County, California. *(Library of Congress, Prints and Photographs Division [HABS,CAL,49-FORO,1A-2])*

began anew, although in 1778, English explorer James Cook went through the Bering Strait several times on visits to Alaska. But Cook did not believe that passage along the Russian Arctic coast was possible, and he did not attempt to sail further west. It was not until 1872 that a serious attempt was made by an Austrian party to find a northeast transit.

Karl Weyprecht and Julius von Payer on the sail-assisted steamship *Tegetthof* set off from Norway in July 1872 to find a passage to the Far East. They intended to try a more northerly route than that of earlier attempts because they had heard that there was open water close to the North Pole. So they headed north, past Novaya Zemlya where they were soon trapped in ice. For more than a year they drifted back and forth, unable to escape. In 1873, they sighted and landed on uncharted terrain that they claimed and named Franz Josef Land. Eventually, they abandoned their ship and managed to safely reach the coast of Norway. Their expedition dispelled the notion that ice conditions were better nearer the Pole.

The voyage of Weyprecht and Payer was studied very carefully by a Swedish geologist and explorer, Nils Adolf Erik Nordenskjöld, who had long had the intention of sailing the Northeast Passage. He had twice sailed from the White Sea to the Yenisei River and felt confident that he could round the infamous Cape Chelyuskin, which had so far defied all explorers, and into the Laptev Sea. From there, he calculated, it would be a month's easy passage to the Bering Strait. With financial aid from private merchant interests and from King Oscar of Sweden he was able to purchase the steamship *Vega* and attending ships, and assemble a competent crew. The *Vega* left Sweden on July 4, 1878, and after difficult but steady progress, reached and passed by Cape Chelyuskin (the most northerly part of Asia, closest to the North Pole at about 77° north lat-

Nils Adolf Erik Nordenskjöld used a steamship, the *Vega*, to traverse the Northeast Passage in little more than a year. *(Library of Congress, Prints and Photographs Division [LC-USZ6-1015])*

itude). The Laptev Sea was at first kind to the travelers, but by September snow was falling, and the patches of ice floes were becoming more and more numerous. Less than one day's steaming from Bering Strait, the *Vega* stopped, unable to move an inch in any direction.

The *Vega* had come to a halt a mile from the mainland; Nordenskjöld soon piled supplies on shore in case the *Vega* had to be given up. As many Arctic explorers before him, he listened to the groaning and cracking of the timbers of his ship and wondered if the vessel could withstand the force of the crushing ice. Meanwhile, he carried out scientific experiments and entertained and traded with the native Chukchi who had flocked to the scene. At Christmas time a tree was fashioned from driftwood and decorated with flags and candles; gifts were given to all the crewmen, and food was parceled out to the Chukchis, who had had a poor hunting season.

Signs of spring eventually appeared: birds, cracks in the ice, and emerging bare spots from the blanket of snow. Then on July 19, 1879, there was a bump, and the *Vega* was free; by the next morning the voyagers were in the middle of Bering Strait. After triumphant stops in Japan, China, Italy, Portugal, England, France, and Denmark, the *Vega* steamed into Stockholm, greeted with the exuberance due the first vessel to sail through the Northeast Passage and pass around the entire Eurasian continent. After some 325 years of attempts, the Northeast Passage had been conquered.

In the many years since Nordenskjöld's historic voyage, the Northeast Passage has undergone incredible development. With the use of massive icebreakers, and then nuclear icebreakers, hundreds of ships now pass through the passage year round. A voyage of 10 days from Murmansk to the Bering Strait is not unusual. Thanks to the Arctic route, the development of the Siberian far north has been a spectacular success.

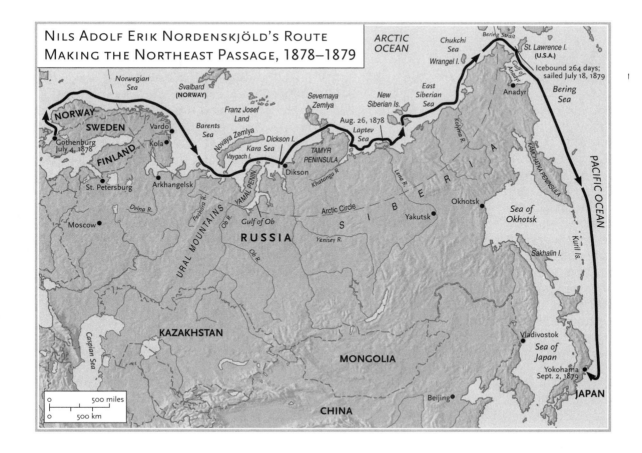

NILS ADOLF ERIK NORDENSKJÖLD'S ROUTE MAKING THE NORTHEAST PASSAGE, 1878–1879

6

THE RACE TO THE NORTH POLE

 In 1850, the search for the lost expedition of Sir John Franklin was in full swing. At this time, no European or American explorer had reached further north than 80° N; the Pole was still some 700 miles beyond. There were several ways by which the search for Franklin spurred Arctic exploration and interest in reaching the North Pole. First, improved navigational skills and better maps and charts made it easier for explorers to plot their journeys and to know where they were and where they were going. Second, the vessels used by the mid-19th century were better designed and built to withstand storms and ice and, with the advent of steam engines, more powerful in getting through frozen Arctic waters. European explorers, in particular the British, began to change their attitudes toward diet, clothing, modes of travel, and the Inuit ways of surviving the Arctic, adapting new methods of cold weather exploration from the same customs they had for so many years looked down upon.

Finally, it is clear that the search for Franklin awakened in Americans the excitement of Arctic exploration. Some participated in the search, and the public showed a keen interest in the exploits of the novice U.S. explorers. Almost immediately the American adventurers turned their attentions to more lofty goals than the finding of Franklin mementoes. In the quest for the Northwest Passage, men's lives and much time had been sacrificed, so the Europeans turned away from the north in frustration. Now the Americans turned their attention, in a very proprietary way, to the North Pole.

AMERICANS TAKE UP THE CHALLENGE

Many of the Americans who tried to reach the North Pole in the second half of the 19th century were affected by an erroneous belief, which geographers and explorers of the time dubbed the "myth of the open polar sea." The idea that there was a ring of ice around the Arctic that, once penetrated, gave way to open water to the North Pole had been around for centuries. Explorers had wanted to believe this geographical improbability because it would allow them to use their ships for Arctic expeditions. The alternative mode of transportation was overland, and in 1850, very few non-natives knew anything about traveling long distances on foot, using sledges to transport all necessities. So it was far preferable to think of finding the right channel and sailing to the Pole than walking there. Whalers and fishermen had returned from Baffin Bay and the coast of Greenland and even further north bringing back stories of open water to the

Shown in this Mathew Brady photograph, Elisha Kent Kane began exploring the Arctic region as a young man and led two expeditions in search of John Franklin. *(National Archives, Still Picture Records, NWDNS-111-B-4192)*

north. These reports reinforced the old belief that one could sail in an open Arctic Ocean, with all the supplies and provisions needed tucked neatly inside the hull of the exploring ship.

Giving weight to the open sea theory were the writings of two 19th-century cartographer-geographers, August Petermann and Matthew Maury. Both of these men had exploration experience, but neither had spent any time in the Arctic. In 1854, Petermann, a German, began a yearly series of studies in geography called *Petermanns Geographische Mitteilungen.* In the first issue, he discussed his theories, formulated several years before, about an open (ice-free) polar ocean. Petermann asserted, "It is a well-known fact that there exists to the north of the Siberian coast a sea open at all seasons; it is beyond doubt that a similar open sea exists on the American side." A few years later, the American naval officer Matthew Maury likewise posited an open polar sea, explaining that a branch of the warm Gulf Stream passed up Davis Strait as an undercurrent and entered the Arctic Ocean. It was partly true—some warm water did empty into the polar sea—but it was not true that the effect of this warm stream was sufficient to cause the Arctic Ocean to remain unfrozen.

American Elisha Kent Kane was one explorer who believed in the open sea theory. Kane had sailed north with Edwin De Haven in 1850 in a search for Franklin. That mission, quickly stalled by icy waters and bad weather, had returned to New York within the year. The mission had failed, but Kane had been caught by the lure of the Arctic, and he vowed to return. At the age of 30, Kane, already had a number of incredible adventures, taken place all over the world, under his belt. He was a most romantic figure; having been stricken at an early age with a serious heart problem, it was as though he was cramming a lifetime of excitement and achievement into the few years of life remaining to him. After his excursion with De Haven, he persuaded Henry Grinnell, a wealthy American businessman, to sponsor another search for Franklin, with himself as commander.

So in May 1853, in De Haven's refurbished ship, the *Advance,* the expedition set forth from New York headed for Baffin Bay. The ostensible purpose of the voyage was to find Franklin's remains. Kane wrote to his brother in August: "The object of my journey is the search after Sir John Franklin: neither science nor the vain glory of attaining an unreached North shall divert me from this one conscientious aim." In fact, Kane's real motive was indeed to sail to the North Pole, but Kane had not chosen his crew well. He had picked up a few unsavory troublemakers at the last minute from the waterfront, and they were later to cause serious trouble for the expedition. In addition, Kane was not a particularly good leader for a hazardous journey into the uncharted north. His health was poor, and he was a terrible seaman, given to bouts of seasickness in bad weather. Furthermore, the *Advance* had not been adequately provisioned: There was food for one year but not enough for two winters.

The *Advance* had rough sailing through the upper reaches of Baffin Bay to Smith Sound. Kane recounted in his diary how the ship was torn free of an iceberg to which it had been anchored:

> August 20, 1853 . . . the strands gave way with the sound of a gun: and we were dragged out by the wild sea, and were at its mercy . . . at seven in the morning we were close upon the piling masses of ice. . . . Down we went with the gale again, helplessly scraping along a lee of ice seldom less than thirty feet thick.

Mathew Brady photographed Elisha Kent Kane (probably center standing) and fellow explorers in their full fur clothing. *(National Archives, Still Picture Records, NWDNS-111-B-4206)*

Along the northwest corner of Greenland, Kane reached land at a harbor that he named Rensselaer Harbor, where the *Advance* became frozen in. Kane describes the food of that terrible winter in his diary: "We divided impartial bites out of the raw hind leg of a fox, to give zest to our biscuits spread with frozen tallow." Kane, despite his frail physical condition, as well as near starvation, scurvy, and the constant threat of mutiny, managed to get through that winter.

In spring 1854, the *Advance* was still frozen in. Kane sent his personal servant, William Morton, on an exploratory trip to the Humboldt Glacier—to date the largest known glacier in North America—to look for the "open sea" that Kane was convinced existed. It is most likely that Morton did not complete the very difficult journey to the top of the glacier, which would have been an ordeal for an experienced and hardy Arctic traveler—which Morton was not. But Morton knew how to stay on the good side of his commander, he returned, reporting that from a vantage point on the northwest coast of Greenland, he had looked north and seen only open water, with "not a speck of ice." It was this promising but untruthful report that kept Kane from retreating south. The *Advance* did not free up in the thaw of summer 1854 and the crew, fed up, openly revolted. Some of the men left the party and headed south on foot. Kane spent the winter of 1854 trying to deal with further mutiny, starvation, scurvy, and his own worsening heart condition. At one point the party began to harvest the ample supply of ship's rats as a food supply. In summer 1855, the remnants of the *Advance,* which had been virtually burned up for fuel, were abandoned, and the crew (rejoined by the deserting mutineers) made its way by the ship's lifeboats to southern Greenland, where they were met by an expedition sent out to search for them.

Kane returned to New York to a hero's welcome. Even though he had no news of Franklin, his claim to have seen the open Arctic Ocean—a mirage, at best—and to have reached farthest north at 80°30' N—an exaggeration—intensified the smoldering American dream of reaching the North Pole by an easy sail beyond the ring of ice. When Kane died of a heart attack in 1857, hundreds of thousands of mourners came to salute the funeral journey from New Orleans to his hometown of Philadelphia.

The quest for the North Pole subsequently began to reach a fever pitch. One of Kane's officers, Isaac Hayes was also an enthusiastic believer in the open polar sea. He was in no way loyal to his commander, Kane, however; Hayes in fact had been the ringleader of the mutineers whom Kane referred to in his journal as a "rotten pack of ingrates." Kane had also written in his diary regarding Hayes, "but-but-but—if I ever live to get home-home! and should meet Dr. Hayes [and the others] let them look out for their skins."

In 1860, Hayes began his exploration aboard the *United States* heading north along the western coast to Greenland. As usual, bad weather and the quickly forming ice took its toll; the party was forced to seek shelter at Etah, on the northwest coast of Greenland. Sledge parties were sent out from Etah (with the help of the Inuit because Hayes's dogs had died of sickness), and Hayes later

Isaac Hayes's claims that he reached the Arctic Ocean during his travels were later proved false. *(Library of Congress, Prints and Photographs Division [LC-USZ62-86623])*

A Sailor's Impressions of the Arctic ⌒

The search for Sir John Franklin gave birth to many fascinating "stepchildren," and one of the most famous of these in its day was the Kane Relief Expedition that went out to search for the second Grinnell Expedition. The latter had taken its name from the wealthy American, Henry Grinnell, who personally paid for much of the expedition's costs. The former took its name from the second Grinnell Expedition's leader, Elisha Kent Kane, a navy surgeon who had already gained a certain celebrity for his various adventures and explorations. Kane's ship had set sail in May 1853, expecting either to find Franklin or to return before the arctic winter set in. When the winter of 1853–54 and then the winter of 1854–55 passed with no word from Kane or his companions, the U.S. Navy decided to send out two ships to search for the Second Grinnell Expedition.

Among those who volunteered for the Kane Relief Expedition was a 20-year-old American seaman, George Cox D'Vys, who had already survived a near drowning at sea. He was made a gunner's mate on the USS *Release,* which set sail from Brooklyn Navy Yard in May 1855. It was not clear how they expected to find Kane and his ship in the vast Arctic seas, but that August they did in fact discover Kane and his men in a small port on an island off Greenland. Kane's own story of survival became a best-selling book.

It is not known whether his shipmates knew that during his time sailing in the Arctic, D'Vys kept a sketchbook in which he drew and painted (with watercolors) scenes he witnessed. He continued to serve in the U.S. Navy and was singled out by Admiral David Porter for his action in the Civil War naval battle of New Orleans. During that time, D'Vys sketched at least one naval engagement in which he fought.

D'Vys left the navy in 1872, and for several years at least he was a contributing illustrator to one of the most popular periodicals of the day, *Frank Leslie's Illustrated Weekly.* He gained no reputation, however, for his artwork, and eventually his sketchpad with its Arctic scenes was passed down and forgotten by his descendants. It has only recently been brought to light, and although no

claimed to have reached the Arctic Ocean. In his book, published in 1867, *The Open Polar Sea,* Hayes wrote that he "stood upon the shores of the Polar Basin, and that the broad ocean lay at my feet." He also claimed to have reached as far north as 82°30' N. Both of the alleged achievements were subsequently disproved.

The next serious attempt at the North Pole was carried out by a most unlikely newspaper editor from Ohio. Charles Francis Hall, in his capacity as a newspaperman, became fascinated with stories and accounts of arctic life and the mystery of John Franklin's disappearance. This ordinary man, who had never been further north than New England, left his wife

claim need be made for D'Vys as a serious artist, his works have the virtue of being an authentic bit of Americana and add yet another footnote to the story of the search for Sir John Franklin.

This drawing of a ship temporarily trapped on an Arctic iceberg is one of several made by George Cox D'Vys, a young American sailor on a ship sent out in 1855 to look for Elisha Kent Kane's expedition. D'Vys's sketchpad was passed down in his family, and this is the first time that any of these drawings have been published. *(Courtesy of Theresa Woffenden Skaza)*

and two children and went to New York seeking money and sponsorship or any other way of getting to the far north. By July 1860, he had managed to get a lift on a whaling ship to Baffin Island where, at his insistence, he was put ashore without money, resources, or any sensible plans. Hall spent two years on Baffin Island, met an Inuit couple—Joe and Hannah—who were to be by his side until the end of his career, and learned the fundamentals of arctic life and travel. Hall was one of the few Arctic explorers who paid close attention to the Inuit and their ways, be it from a limited point of view, as when he wrote in his *Arctic Researches and Life Among the Esquimaux:* "Oh, that such a noble Christianizing work

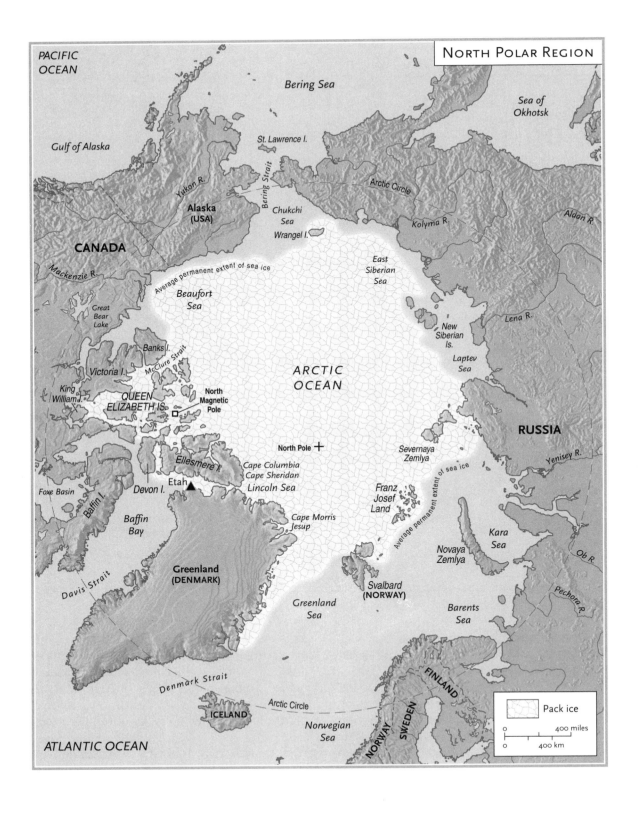

PACIFIC
OCEAN

Bering Sea

Sea of
Okhotsk

Gulf of Alaska

St. Lawrence I.

Arctic Circle

Yukon R.

Alaska
(USA)

Bering Strait

Chukchi
Sea

Wrangel I.

Kolyma R.

Aldan R.

CANADA

East
Siberian
Sea

Mackenzie R.

Average permanent extent of sea ice

Beaufort
Sea

New
Siberian
Is.

Great
Bear
Lake

Lena R.

Banks I.

McClure Strait

Laptev
Sea

Victoria I.

ARCTIC
OCEAN

King
William I.

North
Magnetic
Pole

QUEEN
ELIZABETH IS.

RUSSIA

North Pole ✛

Severnaya
Zemlya

Yenisey R.

Ellesmere I.

Cape Columbia
Cape Sheridan

Franz
Josef
Land

Devon I.

Etah ▲

Lincoln Sea

Foxe Basin

Cape Morris
Jesup

Kara
Sea

Baffin I.

Novaya
Zemlya

Baffin
Bay

Ob R.

Greenland
(DENMARK)

Pechora R.

Davis Strait

Franz Josef Land

Svalbard
(NORWAY)

Barents
Sea

Denmark Strait

Greenland
Sea

FINLAND

Arctic Circle

ICELAND

Norwegian
Sea

SWEDEN

NORWAY

ATLANTIC OCEAN

Average permanent extent of sea ice

Pack ice

0   400 miles

0   400 km

was begun here as is now established in Greenland! . . . Will not some society, some people of civilization, see to this matter ere this noble race passes away?"

Hall returned to the United States in 1862 and spent several years raising money for a return trip to the Arctic. (It is not known how his family survived during these years, since he almost completely neglected them.) Hall returned to the Arctic in 1864 and spent time at Depot Island, Repulse Bay, and King William Island—sites along Canada's northeastern Arctic territory—living with the Inuit and accumulating from them much information about the last days of the Franklin mission. By giving credence to the many Inuit stories and accounts, he was able to find many graves and relics missed by other searchers. Hall's discoveries not only resolved the final chapter in the Franklin saga; they also brought about a new attitude toward the reliability of Inuit testimony.

When Hall returned to the United States in 1869, he was hailed as a hero, and his new fame enabled him to secure the necessary backing for a major expedition to the Arctic with the North Pole as his destination. On July 3, 1871, Hall left New London, Connecticut, in command of the *Polaris,* with a crew of 14 and Joe and Hannah. Hall proceeded north, past his familiar Baffin Island (he was a wiser and more experienced man now) into Baffin Bay and onward north to the dangerous Smith Sound. Passing easily through Smith Sound, which had frustrated many whaling and exploration ships, he moved into Kane Basin, reaching territory visited by Kane and Hayes before him. Passing on, though now meeting hardship such as scurvy, cold, and serious crew dissension, Hall entered Kennedy Channel, the Hall Basin, and the Robeson Channel, waterways between Ellesmere Island and Greenland. The *Polaris* began nearing the

northeastern tip of Ellesmere Island, territory only ever visited by Inuit. On August 30, 1871, the *Polaris* reached 82°11' N—the farthest north ever achieved by an Arctic explorer. But as he was approaching the Lincoln Sea (off the northeastern tip of Ellesmere Island and part of the Arctic Ocean), the ice finally closed in, and Hall was forced to retreat to the northwestern coast of Greenland and find safe winter shelter at a place he named Thank-God Harbor. Shortly thereafter, Hall was given a cup of coffee apparently laced with a massive dose of arsenic, and he soon died. His murder was presumed, but not proven, to be by the ship's doctor, Emil Bessels. The return of the crew of the *Polaris* to civilization, floating on an ice floe from October 15, 1871, to April 29, 1872, for 1,800 miles, is one of the most incredible stories of Arctic survival.

RENEWED EFFORTS

Oddly enough, the experiences of Kane, Hayes, and Hall did little to discourage belief in the far-fetched idea of the open polar sea. The president of the American Geographical and Statistical Society, Charles P. Daly, in a public address, ridiculed the notion that there was open water around the Pole. In 1870, he backed his arguments up with good scientific evidence, but Daly's views were not given much attention in the United States, and in England, they were completely dismissed. The Royal Geographical Society and the Royal Navy felt they could do what the Americans had failed to do. An experienced Arctic explorer, George Strong Nares, was chosen to command an expedition to the North Pole in 1875.

Nares had seen service under Edward Belcher in the search for Franklin and had done work at that time that had given him valuable experience in Arctic travel and survival. He had also done some exploring in Antarctica. Nares was influenced (as was the British Admiralty) by Hayes's erroneous claim to have seen the open polar sea. Although Nares was a competent seaman and leader, and although he was able to obtain a worthy, reliable set of officers and crewmen, the voyage was doomed to failure, because of the incompetence of the Admiralty's preparation. One oversight, among others, was the omission of scurvy-preventive food so that by early 1876, there were several men dead and 60 ill from scurvy. Nonetheless the *Alert* reached a latitude of 82°27' N (along the Lincoln Sea, near Cape Sheridan), before it was frozen in. Sledge parties were sent out, a challenging task as the sledges were too small and poorly made, there were no dogs, the men had no snowshoes, and no one knew how to build a snowhouse. One of the sledge parties was under the command of a capable and persevering young officer named Lieutenant Albert Markham. Many of Markham's group were suffering from scurvy and snow blindness. His party not only had to struggle with the heavy, ill constructed sledges; they were also saddled with a massive boat that they had no use for. Against all odds Markham reached 83°20' N, achieving the farthest-north point ever in exploration up to that time. Markham's party returned to the *Alert* in dire condition, with half of his men barely able to walk. Although the expedition had been expected to last two years, Nares wisely retreated when the spring thaw arrived and returned to England in November 1876. His sponsors were somewhat disappointed by the outcome of the expedition, although it had accomplished one definite benefit: There was not much belief anymore that the North Pole was surrounded by ice-free water.

Yet there were still a few explorers who would not give up the dream that the Pole could be reached by sailing through open water. A young lieutenant in the U.S. Navy, George Washington DeLong, was one of them. He was an admirer of the theories of Karl Weyprecht, a German naval officer who had tried but failed to find the warm current that must flow unfrozen through the Arctic Ocean. DeLong believed that Weyprecht had started from the wrong side of the Arctic and was convinced that he could find the open water to the Pole if he started from the Bering Strait. DeLong, against all advice, purchased an unsuitable vessel, the *Jeanette*, and hired himself a crew consisting of officers of no Arctic experience, American Indians rather than Inuit, and troublemakers from the waterfront. The expedition was sponsored by James Gordon Bennett, Jr., of the *New York Herald* (the same publisher who had sponsored Henry Stanley's search for David Livingstone in Africa in 1869–71), and the whole endeavor had a circuslike atmosphere about it. DeLong himself was lacking in experience and certainly was not a scientist; the expedition was to be an adventure.

The adventure did not last long after the *Jeanette* party left California in summer 1879. By September the expedition passed through the Bering Strait and froze in the pack ice east of Wrangel Island in the Chukchi Sea, north of Russia's Siberian coast. A year later, in 1880, the *Jeanette* was still solidly frozen in, having drifted northeast and north and then back again to where they began. The temperature stood that December at –50° Fahrenheit and the latitude was 74° 41' N, nowhere near the Pole. Fuel was running out, and the ship was beginning to break up under the pressure. DeLong betrayed his concern when he recorded in his journal of this time: "[M]y motto is, 'Hope on, hope ever.' A very good one it is when one's surroundings are more natural than ours; but situated as we are, it is better in the abstract than in realization."

Eventually the *Jeanette* was abandoned, and almost all supplies were left on board, to sink with the ship. After further mishaps, three of the ship's boats started for the mainland of Siberia. One boat sank with all hands; a second boat, commanded by Lieutenant Melville, reached the delta of the Lena River in northern Siberia, and the men were rescued; the third, DeLong's boat, reached a part of the delta where there were no settlements. His party died one by one. DeLong's last diary entry reads: "October 30th, Sunday. Boyd and Goertz died during the night, Mr. Collins dying." A hypothetical date for DeLong's death is November 1, 1881. Years later, relics from the *Jeanette* were found on the southwest coast of Greenland. Ironically, the *Jeanette* must have drifted eastward all the way across the Arctic Ocean.

By the time news of the DeLong disaster reached the United States, plans were already under way for another attempt at the Pole. As part of the International Polar Year (1882–83), an international and cooperative effort to direct polar exploration and research away from nationalistic ends, the Americans had agreed to maintain a polar station and to gather and exchange data and information with other participants and the general science community. In fact, what the Americans planned to do was to go further north than any explorer had ever gone ("farthest north") and to reach the Pole, if possible. The expedition was formed by the U.S. military under the command of Major Adolphus A. W. Greely. By summer 1882 Greely had established a base off the Hall Basin that he named Fort Conger, and with his lieutenant, James B. Lockwood, established a new farthest north by four miles. Troubles soon beset the mission; discipline broke down, and a crewman was shot for stealing food. A supply ship was to arrive with supplies for the winter of 1882–83 but it did

Major Adolphus A. W. Greely and some of his crew survived a disastrous mission, which entailed abandoning their ships to live in Greenland until whalers arrived to rescue them two years after their ordeal began. *(Library of Congress, Prints and Photographs Division [LC-USZ62-95948])*

not appear then, nor in 1883. The desperate, starving men abandoned their ship for the boats and retreated south to Cape Sabine, very near Etah, Greenland, and civilization. There they remained, fighting and squabbling with one another, living on the occasional fox or seal and scraping of lichens from rock. Discipline and order were gone; exposure, starvation, and scurvy claimed one man after another. When rescuing whalers arrived in June 1884, the remaining party was huddled half-conscious in their shelter, an overturned

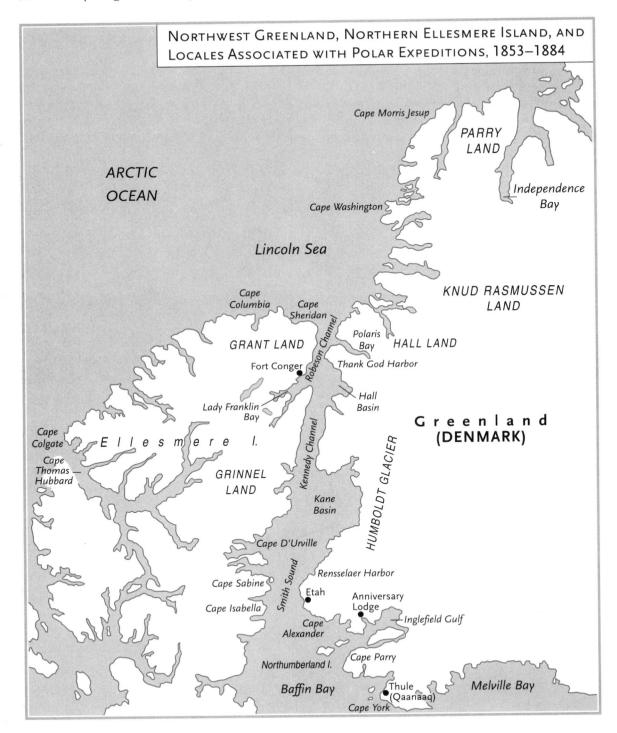

NORTHWEST GREENLAND, NORTHERN ELLESMERE ISLAND, AND
LOCALES ASSOCIATED WITH POLAR EXPEDITIONS, 1853–1884

Cape Morris Jesup

PARRY
LAND

ARCTIC
OCEAN

Independence
Bay

Cape Washington

Lincoln Sea

KNUD RASMUSSEN
LAND

Cape
Columbia

Cape
Sheridan

Polaris
Bay

HALL LAND

GRANT LAND

Robeson Channel

Fort Conger

Thank God Harbor

Lady Franklin
Bay

Hall
Basin

Greenland
(DENMARK)

Cape
Colgate

Ellesmere I.

Cape
Thomas
Hubbard

Kennedy Channel

GRINNEL
LAND

Kane
Basin

HUMBOLDT GLACIER

Cape D'Urville

Rensselaer Harbor

Cape Sabine

Etah

Anniversary
Lodge

Cape Isabella

Smith Sound

Inglefield Gulf

Cape
Alexander

Northumberland I.

Cape Parry

Baffin Bay

Thule
(Qaanaaq)

Melville Bay

Cape York

boat. Of the 26 members of the party, six men and Greely survived.

EUROPEANS RETURN TO THE QUEST

A different kind of attempt at the Pole was made by Norwegian explorer and scientist Fridtjof Nansen, often called the "father of modern Arctic oceanography." Nansen's first great feat, in 1888, was crossing the Greenland ice cap from east to west, beating out American explorer Robert Peary, who had planned to accomplish this feat himself. The crossing was not an easy one; Nansen, in his usual droll way, described in his journal how in desperate hunger he ate an extra pair of snowshoes—hide, wood, and all. But Nansen was not immune to the lure of the Arctic. As he expressed in his book, *The First Crossing of Greenland,* "I am sure that our nocturnal marches over the Inland Ice of Greenland made an ineradicable impression upon all of us who were on that expedition."

Nansen had long been intrigued by the mystery of the circumpolar ice drift. He believed that an ice current moved slowly around the North Pole and that a ship frozen into the polar pack north of Siberia, if it could avoid being crushed, would drift in the ice near the Pole or even over it. To test his theory, he designed and built a special ship, the *Fram* (Norwegian for "forward") with a round bottom that, when frozen in the ice pack, would rise up and sit on top of the ice rather than be crushed by it. The *Fram* would then serve as a "floating" oceanographic laboratory; it was stocked with enough supplies to sustain the explorers for up to five years.

In June 1892, the *Fram* departed Oslo, Norway, and in September merged with the polar ice pack at the New Siberian Islands at 77°44' N. The rudder was hauled up, and the engine was removed and packed in oil to prevent rusting. The crew members set themselves to numerous scientific projects involving marine life and oceanographic observations. Nansen reported in his journal that they were on a "luxury cruise" and the "the men grew fat as pigs." A typical dinner one night was canned tongue, bacon, ham, caviar, potatoes, and baked cauliflower, followed by desert—honey cake, pineapple, figs, and strawberries. Everything was washed down with beer. After dinner there was a cigar for everyone. The *Fram* performed perfectly; it sat like a castle on top of the ice, largely unaffected by the grinding and smashing going on beneath it.

Fridtjof Nansen built a special ship with a rounded bottom, the *Fram*, to explore the area near the North Pole. *(Library of Congress, Prints and Photographs Division [LC-USZ62-100825])*

Eventually, however, it became apparent the *Fram* was not going to drift near to the Pole. Nansen, leaving the ship under the command of Otto Sverdrup, struck out by ski and sledge for the North Pole with Hjalmar Johansen, dogs, and 1,400 pounds of supplies. At 86°13.6' N, 200 miles from their goal, Nansen and Johansen were forced to retreat. With great difficulty, and suffering much hardship, the pair trekked to a settlement on Franz Josef Land—a group of islands well within the Arctic Circle—from which they were rescued and reunited with Sverdrup and the *Fram*. All returned in 1896 to Oslo in triumph.

Meanwhile, in the United States, as the 19th century was drawing to a close, the ardor for polar exploration had cooled down. Not just the failure but the deadly conclusions of the expeditions of Hall, DeLong, and Greely had brought apprehensions to the minds of would-be explorers and stilled the enthusiasm of the general public. In addition, the

Fridtjof Nansen's funeral procession following his death in 1930 demonstrates the great respect and admiration of the Norwegian people for this great explorer. *(Library of Congress, Prints and Photographs Division [LC-USZ62-128548])*

myth of the open polar sea had been cast out, meaning that if the Pole could not be reached by ship then a whole new way of traveling in the Arctic would have to be undertaken. Interestingly, it was an Italian mission in 1900 that was one of the first to accept the fact that travel in the Arctic must be based on dogs and not ships. Luigi Amedeo, duke of the Abruzzi, leader of the expedition, passed command to his captain, Umberto Cagni, who with three companions traveled with sled dogs from Franz Josef Land to 86°34' N, a bit farther north than Nansen's record. The party had managed a good speed and showed its ability to move over very rough sea ice.

This expedition, although it did not reach the Pole, proved the greater efficiency of dogs over men for hauling supplies over the ice. Furthermore, it finally implemented the tried-and-true, centuries-old methods of the Inuit, bringing to an end 200 years of such ill-suited exploration techniques as traveling with horses, mules, and even reindeer. Another fact was brought to light by the somewhat obscure expedition of Umberto Cagni: Franz Josef Land and Spitsbergen were not good jumping-off sites for a polar attempt because they were too far from the Pole and too remote and hard to get to. The Canadian, not the Eurasian side of the Arctic must therefore be the starting area.

The Hall, DeLong, and Greely fiascos plus the Abruzzi advances had made the future very clear: The Arctic was no place for dabblers and adventurers and opportunists. The explorer who would achieve the prize of the North Pole would be a person driven by a passion so intense that the desperate hardship of the quest would not—could not—weaken his resolve. Such an individual must be prepared to battle the Arctic on its own terms. There would be no organs and dramatic performances, no libraries, no caviar, and no cigars after dinner. It would be man against nature, and man against all within him that would compromise his will to strive and conquer. Robert Edwin Peary was such a man.

ROBERT PEARY'S QUEST

At the age of 30, Robert Peary had traveled to Greenland as a naval officer, and from that moment on, he dedicated himself to a career in Arctic exploration. During the 1890s, Peary made six expeditions to Greenland, all with the goal of finding the best route to the North

Robert E. Peary stands on the deck of the *Roosevelt* in full fur clothing. *(Library of Congress, Prints and Photographs Division [LC-USZ62-8234])*

Robert E. Peary, who learned much from the Inuit as did many other explorers, distributed gifts to some Inuit from the deck of a ship. *(Library of Congress, Prints and Photographs Division [LC-USZ62-30426])*

Pole. In 1904, he sailed on a specially designed ship, the *Roosevelt*, determined to reach the Pole. Two years later, Peary floated into New York aboard the badly damaged *Roosevelt*, defeated in his second attempt at reaching the North Pole. Peary was not discouraged; rather, his determination rose to a new height of intensity. His whole being and purpose in life focused with greater intensity on attaining his goal of the North Pole: He

would either reach it in the next attempt or die in the trying.

In 1908, Peary was no longer a young man —he was 52—and he was scarred and crippled by the struggles and ordeals of 30 years of exploration. He felt that he had given up everything for his quest: a naval career, a serene life with his family, and the pleasures and contentment that might come from a life of achieving more reasonable goals. Shrugging

A Tragic Attempt at the Pole from Above

At about the same time Robert Peary was making his second expedition to Greenland, another was being launched by a Swedish engineer named Solomon August Andrée. Andrée planned to fly over the North Pole in a balloon. He had had considerable experience with this mode of travel, but he was not at all familiar with the Arctic and the grave dangers inherent in the severe weather there. In 1896, after raising the requisite finances, he traveled by ship to an island off the coast of Spitsbergen, the main island in the Svalbard group of islands north of Norway. He had ready his equipment that included a hydrogen generator with which to inflate his balloon, but a crucial favorable wind never came and he returned to Sweden.

Although unfamiliar with the Arctic, Andrée knew enough about ballooning to be aware of the folly of his attempt. He knew that the polar wind did not flow over the Pole; he also knew that, once aloft, he would be utterly at the mercy of the erratic and highly changeable winds. And he must have realized that any trouble that caused the balloon to come down would put the flyers in a dire position on the polar ice. Andrée did show some apprehension; he wrote in his diary: "Shall we be thought mad or will our example be followed?"

The following summer, 1897, Andrée returned to Spitsbergen to try again. In the interim, Andrée had designed a hanging rope system that when dragged along the ice, allowed the direction of aircraft to be controlled by the crew; it seemed unlikely to all that this method of dealing with the arctic wind could possibly work. Nonetheless, when the wind was right, on July 11, 1897, Andrée and his two companions cut the restraining ropes and the *Ornen* rose (after nearly plunging in the sea) high in the sky and disappeared. Several days later a whaling ship captured a homing pigeon released from the balloon with a message that reported that 82° N had been reached and all was well.

The rest of the story was learned from Andrée's diary, which was found 30 years later. The balloon drifted to the northeast, then to the west, and then to the east. The guide ropes had broken free in the ascent, so no control was possible. Andrée wrote that he soon realized that they would never make it to the Pole. Then, a heavy fog descended, and the balloon was unable to float more than a few feet above the ice. After banging from ice ridge to ice ridge for three days, the *Ornen* landed. The expedition was at 83° N, without any hope of rescue. The decision was made to walk to Franz Josef Land, where supplies were cached. Inexperienced at navigation and inadequately equipped, the three men missed their destination. Their remains and Andrée's diary were discovered by later explorers in a shelter where there seemed to be an abundance of food.

off the disappointment that might have broken a lesser man, Peary set about preparing for his final assault on the Pole. Peary had done his preparatory work well: He had participated in seven major expeditions from 1886 to 1905, either to Greenland or toward the Pole. He knew the route that must be taken, and he realized that the starting point must be from the northernmost point of Ellesmere Island, Cape Columbia. He knew the dangers of the changing seasons and had figured out the narrow window that existed between the freezing of the ice and the dangerous thawing in the spring that opened up

leads. And Peary, more than any other American explorer of his time, knew that he must use fully the Inuit ways of travel, eating, shelter building, clothing, and most of all, the skillful use of dogs. Also, Peary had perfected a system of ferrying supplies by support teams: retreating for pick-ups, advancing with needed food and fuel, then falling back to be replaced by others. One by one, the supporting teams would drop off and return to the *Roosevelt,* anchored at Cape Sheridan. A small party only, would make the dash to the Pole. There were to be five support teams led by Robert Bartlett, Ross Marvin, Dr. John

Robert Bartlett (right) led one of the support teams that helped Robert E. Peary (left) and Matthew Henson reach the North Pole in 1909. *(Library of Congress, Prints and Photographs Division [LC-USZ62-119801])*

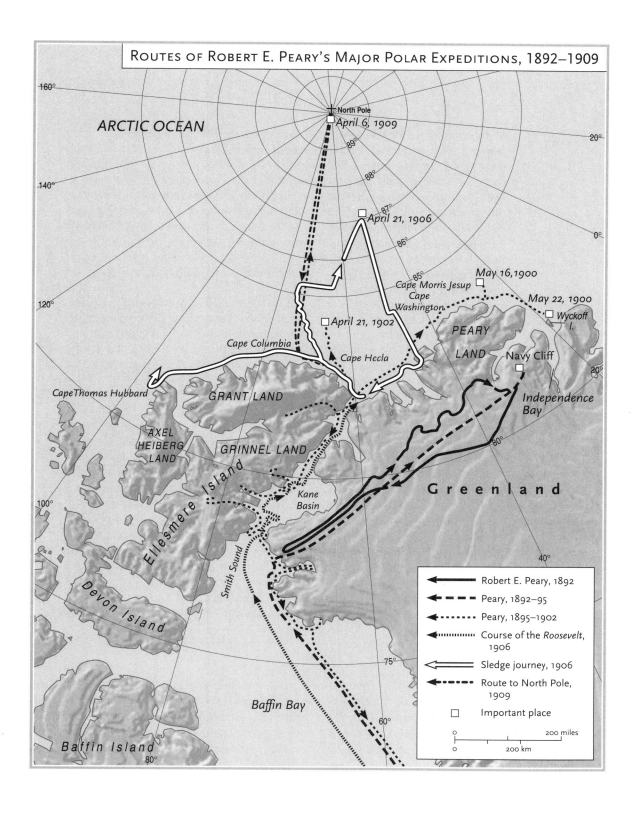

ROUTES OF ROBERT E. PEARY'S MAJOR POLAR EXPEDITIONS, 1892–1909

160°

ARCTIC OCEAN

140°

120°

100°

North Pole
April 6, 1909

89°
88°
87° — April 21, 1906
86°
85°

Cape Morris Jesup — May 16, 1900
Cape Washington
May 22, 1900
Wyckoff I.

PEARY LAND

April 21, 1902
Cape Columbia
Cape Hecla
Navy Cliff

CapeThomas Hubbard
GRANT LAND
Independence Bay

AXEL HEIBERG LAND
GRINNEL LAND
Greenland

Ellesmere Island
Kane Basin

Smith Sound
Devon Island

Baffin Bay

80°
40°
75°
60°

Baffin Island

20°

0°

20°

20°

80°

Robert E. Peary, 1892
Peary, 1892–95
Peary, 1895–1902
Course of the *Roosevelt*, 1906
Sledge journey, 1906
Route to North Pole, 1909
◻ Important place

0 — 200 miles
0 — 200 km

Miy Paluk

Matt Henson was born in 1866 to a black sharecropping family in Maryland. He was orphaned at 11 and apparently spent a few years on the streets of Washington, D.C., completely on his own. At 13 he went to sea as a cabin boy and rose to the rank of able-bodied seaman in six years. Between jobs, he was working as a stock clerk in a hat shop when Robert Peary hired him. Henson was recommended to Peary for his industry and his reliability; Peary was looking for a personal valet for his explorations, and it was to Henson's advantage that although young, he was an experienced sailor. Henson went on to accompany Peary on seven of his eight missions, including his final voyage and conquest of the North Pole. On April 6, 1909, Robert Peary and Matthew Henson stood together at the North Pole.

Through the 17 years of Peary's and Henson's shared endeavors, their relationship remained, in every sense, that of servant and master. Despite the many times their lives lay in each other's hands, despite the deadly dangers met and overcome together, Henson was never permitted to think of himself as a companion or a fellow explorer. There is no question, however, that Henson was a valuable member of the various Arctic teams.

Donald MacMillan, an explorer in the final polar quest, wrote later in regard to Henson's experience and skills that "he was of more real value than the combined services of all of us." In the 1908 final attempt, Henson served as sledge builder, driver, hunter, carpenter, blacksmith, and cook. Then there were his other duties as valet: cooking breakfast every morning for his boss, taking care of his clothing and gear, ministering to his personal needs, and coming to his aid when his injured leg gave way. Peary never showed gratitude to Henson for his efforts and abilities; apparently, he was afraid of creating dissension within the party if he gave any indication that Henson had status. He took to referring to Henson in derogatory terms to ensure that Henson knew and accepted his place. Henson wrote in his diary that he consoled himself by reading the Bible. "And the meek shall inherit the earth" from the book of Matthew was his favorite text.

To Peary, Henson was "my colored boy" and "my dark-skinned kinky haired child of the Equator." To the Inuit, Henson was Miy Paluk, or "dear Matty." Hen-

Goodsell, George Borup, and Dr. Donald MacMillan. Each of these men was assigned several Inuit dog drivers and from 16 to 24 dogs. Matthew (Matt) Henson, Peary's African-American manservant, was an excellent driver and was also given a dog team. But because Henson's status was that of a servant, not an explorer or scientist, he was not designated a team leader. His services and his dogs, were under the direct command of Peary.

The organization worked out. The first units left Cape Columbia on February 28,

son was truly loved by the Inuit because he was a great hunter and dog driver, because he had learned to speak their language, and because he treated them with affection and respect. When the Inuit parted from Maktok Kabloona (black white man), they told him he would be remembered forever for his kindness and strength.

After Peary returned to triumph from the North Pole, he had little further to do with Henson. A brusque dismissal and the $25-a-month expedition salary ended their association. Peary's only subsequent public reference to his valet was some disparaging comments about his competence.

Henson returned to a job in a parking lot; later he became a messenger, earning $17 a week. In 1912, Henson published his autobiography, *A Black Explorer at the North Pole*. When he was 71, he was given a membership in the famous Explorers Club. It is not known if he ever went there; it is said that he could not afford the price of lunch. In 1944, the U.S. Congress awarded him a joint medal for his work on the expedition. The Geographical Society of Chicago gave him their gold medal in 1948. Matthew Henson died in 1955. Not until 1988 was he reburied in Arlington National Cemetery with military honors, a late but fitting recognition of his achievements.

Matthew Henson fulfilled many roles as Robert E. Peary's personal valet; together, they reached the North Pole on April 6, 1909. *(Library of Congress, Prints and Photographs Division [LC-USZ62-42993])*

1909, and by April 1, Peary had reached 87°47' N, 133 miles from the Pole. The last team, led by "Cap'n Bob" (Bartlett), retreated to base camp, and only Peary, Henson, and four Inuit guides remained. On April 6, 1909, this small band reached the North Pole; Peary made solar observations and Henson took 110 photographs. Peary expressed his feelings in his book, *The North Pole:* "The pole at last!!! The prize of three centuries, my dreams and ambitions for twenty-three years. *Mine* at last. I cannot bring myself

Robert Peary built these quarters in northern Greenland as a base camp from which he and his support teams began their approach to the North Pole. *(Library of Congress, Prints and Photographs Division [LC-USZ62-128546])*

to realize it. It all seems so simple and commonplace."

After three days, the explorers began the return to the *Roosevelt.* It was a difficult retreat; there was much trouble with leads that were opening in the water, but the return was amazingly swift. While returning to New York from Ellesmere Island, Peary learned that his arch-competitor, Dr. Frederick Cook, had claimed to have reached the Pole on April 21, 1908—almost a year earlier.

THE COOK CLAIM

Cook, a fellow American, had been on an Arctic mission under Peary in 1891–92, but the two men did not get on well at all. Cook had signed on for a second expedition in 1893,

but an altercation with Peary brought a breach between the two men that was never healed. While Peary went off to Greenland, Cook remained behind and worked to further his own plans for exploration in the Arctic. Cook spent the next several years as an Arctic guide, working mainly in the Greenland area. In 1897, he was appointed medical officer aboard the *Belgica,* bound for exploration in Antarctica under the command of Adrien de Gerlache, a Belgian who had organized the expedition on his own. One of the young officers on the *Belgica* was Roald Amundsen, who reported later that Cook won the respect and devotion of all hands because of his hard work and his constant attention to the health and well-being of his comrades.

In 1907, Cook was a member of a hunting safari to northern Greenland, sponsored by a wealthy American sportsman-hunter, John R. Bradley. He persuaded Bradley to finance an attempt at the Pole. When the hunting was over, Cook remained in Etah, Greenland; on February 19, 1908, Cook started on his expedition to the Pole with two Inuit, two sledges, and 26 dogs. This expedition crossed Ellesmere Island to the east coast, and then headed northwest along Alex Heiberg Island. Without any particular setbacks—all this according to Cook's own account—he proceeded to the North Pole, reaching it on April 21, 1908. Cook maintained that he then retreated south to Devon Island and spent the winter there, returning to his starting point, Etah, in May 1909.

There, in Etah, Cook maintained that he left his instruments and navigation notes in the safe-keeping of Harry Whitney, another wealthy American hunter. Later, some instruments were found, but no notes authenticating his route and his celestial navigation. In fact, Cook was never able to produce the evidence to show that he had traveled from Alex Heiberg Island to the Pole. The acclaim with which Cook was greeted when he arrived in Copenhagen was tempered from the beginning with doubt. Although he was cheered in a parade in his native city, Brooklyn, by 100,000 people in late 1909, the relentless attack upon his claims was kept up by Robert Peary and his rich and influential supporters. Claims and evidence presented by Cook were one by one proven false. In October 1909, Cook disap-

Explorers often built shelters of ice such as this one photographed somewhere along Frederick Cook's expedition to the North Pole. *(Library of Congress, Prints and Photographs Division [LC-USZ62-103156])*

In this 1911 photograph, Frederick Cook (right) and an unidentified man wear fur clothing in front of an Arctic backdrop. *(Library of Congress, Prints and Photographs Division [LC-USZ62-119526])*

peared from New York and was not seen for 10 months. When he returned to the United States in 1910, Cook told a reporter, "I still believe I reached the Pole although I am not sure I did." By the end of 1910, Cook's claim to the Pole was essentially discredited.

In the decades since, scholars and historians have continued to wage a battle over which of these men—Peary or Cook—first reached the North Pole. The most recent prevailing opinion is that neither explorer reached it at all. Faulty navigation, overzealousness, or outright deception have been attributed to both explorers. It is bitterly ironic that the attainment of the North Pole, and the extraordinary endeavor required to do so, is and will be forever clouded in doubt and suspicion.

The Inuit term for the North Pole when translated into English means "the big nail." The image to them was a gigantic piece of iron reaching to the sky in the midst of the Arctic waste. A big nail, an everlasting supply of the material most precious and life-sustaining to the native people of the north: How else could they begin to understand what motivated the Americans and Europeans to want to reach the most dangerous, most remote, most lifeless, and the most worthless part of the frozen desert? Perhaps there is no rational, satisfying explanation for the lure of the North Pole and willingness of explorers to dedicate their lives to the achievement of this intangible goal. Perhaps it is enough to note that generations of explorers gave their lives to the discovery of what might lie ahead, over the cold, bleak horizon. Their deaths may have come about through vanity, folly, or ignorance, but each failed expedition laid the groundwork for the next until the prize was won. From this point of view, the Cook-Peary dispute is subsumed by the collective manifestation or unconquerable will that is the ultimate spirit of exploration.

7

EXPLORING ANTARCTICA

The Antarctic expedition of James Clark Ross (1839–43) with the *Erebus* and the *Terror* can stand as a symbol of the excitement and exhilaration of the discovery of the hidden continent, Antarctica. A number of other explorers had seen the towering height of icy mountains and the barren rocky peaks that rose even higher, but none had stood in the presence of the terrible and awesome beauty that presented itself to Ross as he landed on an island in 1841 (later to be named after him). First, there is always a unique thrill of beholding that which has never before been seen by human eye. Then, the sheer magnificence of the Transantarctic Mountains, stretching to the limit of sight toward the South Pole, presented a vista of pristine majesty. Like so many explorers in the region before them, Ross and his party were struck by the coincidence of natural beauty and the power of nature, and thoughts about humans and their relationship to nature and a deity inevitably came to mind. Even the blacksmith, Cornelius Sullivan, wrote in his journal, "There is a sort of awe that steals over us all considering our own insignificance and helplessness."

As the party sailed west along the shore, Dr. Robert McCormick, the expedition's surgeon, saw what appeared to be a fine snow-

By sailing the *Erebus* and *Terror* along the continent's edge, James Clark Ross explored more of the Antarctic region than had anyone before him. *(Library of Congress, Prints and Photographs Division [LC-USZ62-85688])*

James Clark Ross and his crew explored such features as what was later named in his honor the Ross Ice Shelf. *(Library of Congress, Prints and Photographs Division [LC-USZ62-101004])*

drift. He wrote in his diary, January 28, 1841: "As we made a nearer approach, however, this apparent snowdrift resolved itself into a dense column of smoke, intermingled with flakes of red flame, emerging from a magnificent volcanic vent, in the very center of a mountain range encased in eternal ice and snow." They named it on the spot Mount Erebus, after the expedition ship, and a nearby peak was named Mount Terror. Soon after, the explorers came upon a perpendicular cliff of ice, 120 to 250 feet high, flat on top and composed of solid ice, as smooth as glass; it rose straight up from the sea and had not one crack, fissure, or opening in it. It would become known as the

Ross Ice Shelf. It seemed more impregnable and unscalable than anything that could ever be constructed by human agency. Nearby, out to sea, the raging ocean tossed gigantic chunks of pack ice against mountain-sized icebergs, fragmenting them into a million pieces of glittering crystal. Great herds of whales cavorted and dove around the ships. Ross noted in his diary a sad prediction about these whales that "had enjoyed a life of tranquility beyond the reach of persecutors, but would soon be made to contribute to the wealth of our country."

Soon it was February and the antarctic winter was approaching. By mid-March, the

Erebus and the *Terror* had fought free of the re-forming ice pack and were retreating to Hobart, Tasmania, a safe harbor for the winter. Ross returned to Antarctica November 1841–March 1842 and again December 1842–March 1843; although these voyages produced no major discoveries, they sailed along different sections of the coast, identified a number of new landmarks, and produced more charts and geographical data. The *Erebus* and the *Terror* finally arrived back in England in September 1843; not a single member of the expedition had been lost. Every conceivable honor was heaped upon Sir James Clark Ross, and the exploration was deemed a complete success.

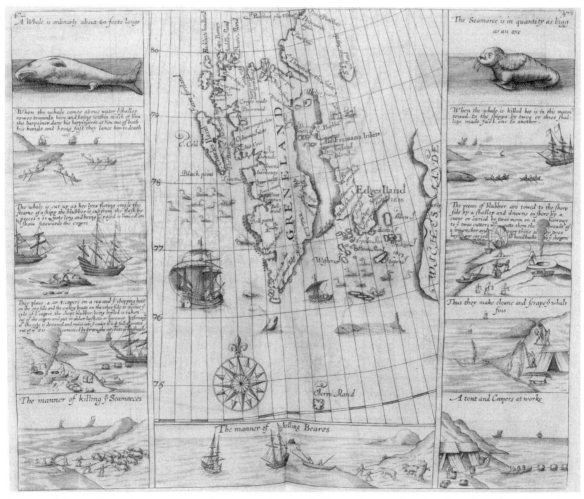

Arctic and Antarctic exploration opened the areas to the whaling industry. This drawing illustrates the early industry as established in Greenland. *(National Library of Canada)*

IN THE WAKE OF ROSS

All of the Antarctic explorers of this era—James Weddell, Jules-Sébastien-César Dumont d'Urville, Charles Wilkes—had seen such sights as Ross saw. And all reported on the incredible beauty of the southern continent. But all also saw no future in this terrible land where no human settlement could ever be possible—or at least practical. Consequently, once Antarctica had been located and seen for what it was, further attempts at exploration in the last half of the 19th century were few. The only adventurers to be found in the southern ocean were the whalers, and they were not interested in discovery. They were, as Ross predicted, after the enormous profits reaped by slaughtering the whale herds—in some cases, to extinction.

During the middle decades of the 1800s, the British became occupied with the search for the missing Franklin expedition in the Arctic. Americans turned their attentions to the Civil War and the aftermath of the nation-dividing strife during the Reconstruction period. In neither the Old World nor the new had anyone figured out how to turn Antarctica into a profit. The phase of exploration that involved *finding* the hidden continent probably came to a close when on January 24, 1895, a small party from a Norwegian whale-hunting ship landed on Cape Adare (near the Ross Ice Shelf). With the landing party were the expedition's manager, Henryk Bull, the ship's captain, Leonard Kristensen; and its first mate, Carsten Borchgrevink (the latter would claim that he was the first human to set foot on Antarctica, although a 17-year-old sailor, Alexander von Tunzelman, insisted that he had actually jumped out first to steady the boat).

That same year, an occurrence provided great impetus to exploration in the Antarctic and proposed that exploration would not be based on a profit motive: In 1895, in London, the Congress of the International Geographical Union urged that scientific teams be sent there "in view of the vast addition to knowledge which would result." It is important to note that the congress stressed science and knowledge as the end of exploration and international teamwork as a means of international cooperation. These characteristics have prevailed in almost all efforts and exploration in Antarctica since the pronouncements of the 1895 congress.

Just a year before the meeting of the congress, a young Belgian navy lieutenant, Adrien de Gerlache, had written a paper recommending a Belgian expedition to Antarctica. Because the stated objectives of the proposed voyage were specifically scientific, Gerlache had difficulty in securing financial backing. He spent his time alternately in raising funds and studying methods of sledging and types of proper clothing and equipment. Finally, in August 1897, Gerlache left Belgium aboard the *Belgica* and reached Cape Horn in 1898; from there he continued south to the tip of the Antarctic Peninsula. The *Belgica* moved south along Graham Land, following the coast (to the west) of the Antarctic Peninsula. Several times a day crew members, on boats, would go ashore and gather specimens of rocks, plants, and the few wingless insects that inhabit Antarctica. Still heading south, along Palmer Land, Gerlache attempted to reach Alexander Land, probably because he wanted to best Captain James Cook's farthest point south of 71° S (in 1774), or even Ross's of 78° S. But inevitably, the ice closed in in March 1898 at the beginning of Antarctica's winter, and at 71°22' S (300 miles inside the Antarctic Circle), the *Belgica* was imprisoned for 347 days. Gerlache and his crew thus became the first to spend a winter inside the continental ice pack of Antarctica, albeit offshore of the mainland.

A great deal of scientific work was carried out over the next year, but the first wintering in Antarctica took a terrible toll on the explorers. Constant darkness, deep cold, and isolation plunged the members of the party into severe depression and psychological instability. Two officers became towers of strength in maintaining morale and order: Roald Amundsen and Frederick Cook, both of whom would later achieve fame for their exploits seeking the North and South Poles. In a journal entry reproduced in his book, *Through the First Antarctic Night,* Cook was frank about the experience: "We are imprisoned in an endless sea of ice. . . . We have told all the tales, real or imaginative, to which we are equal. Time weighs heavily upon us as the darkness slowly advances."

In March 1899, the crew freed the *Belgica* from the frozen pack with explosives and ice saws, and the explorers returned to Belgium, bringing with them a wealth of scientific data. Significantly, the valuable information was given freely to the international community, thus setting a precedent for a cooperative spirit that was to characterize future discoveries and findings in the Antarctic.

At about the time that Gerlache was afield, Norwegian explorer Carsten Borchgrevink was conducting scientific research on the other side of the continent. Borchgrevink, who in 1895 claimed to have been the first person to set foot on Antarctica, had determined at that time that he would return to explore Antarctica. Borchgrevink was almost mystical when he explained his motives in his book, *First on the Antarctic Continent:* "Man's philosophy has . . . reached the glittering gates of the poles where eternity rules in stern silence, awaiting the hour when time is ripe through the sacrifice of mortals, for man to be allowed to follow his philosophy and to enter the Polar crystal palaces and to satisfy his thirst for certainty."

He obtained financial support from various private sources and left London in 1898 on the *Southern Cross,* and after a most troublesome voyage, the expedition reached Cape Adare (Victoria Land) in 1899. There, he and nine men built a winter shelter, while the *Southern Cross* retreated to New Zealand. For nine months Borchgrevink did extensive zoological work and, with dogs, explored the nearby regions. In 1900, Borchgrevink explored the Ross Ice Shelf and with William Colbeck traveled by sledge to 78°50' S, establishing a new farthest-south record. Borchgrevink deserves recognition for being the first to winter over on the Antarctic mainland. His data and his charts of the Ross Sea area provided great assistance to later explorers and helped pave the way to the reaching of the South Pole.

In 1895, the Congress of the International Geographical Union had declared that Antarctica was the greatest piece of exploratory work yet to be accomplished. The continent had been found; now it must be "conquered." This was to be the work of the intrepid 20th-century explorers who dared to challenge the most hostile region on Earth.

ANTARCTICA IN THE 20TH CENTURY

Three international expeditions were undertaken in 1901, designated "Antarctic Year" by another international geographical congress. A German geographer, Erich von Drygalski, sponsored by the German government, set sail on the *Gauss* in August 1901. The ship became trapped in ice between February 1902 and February 1903 along the side of Antarctica completely opposite the Antarctic Peninsula.

Dogs and Transport

British explorers traditionally preferred to do their Arctic exploring by ship; this preference held true in the case of exploring Antarctica, too. Consequently, when there was too much ice for the expedition ships to progress, the mission was to a large degree stymied. When exploration overland was required in the first half of the 19th century, the British teams hauled their supplies over the snow and ice on sledges pulled by men. This method turned out to be a most unsatisfactory mode of transport.

The Inuit of North America and the indigenous peoples of Arctic Asia had been using dogs to haul sledges for many hundreds of years. They had developed several breeds, all close descendants of the wolf. These dogs, although thoroughly domesticated, are in fact considered the closest relatives of the wolf of all the dog breeds. It is still a custom in the Arctic to tie a female husky to a stake in the wild so that a "visit" by a wolf will produce pups that have the stamina and characteristics of the father. Most huskies, however, are not savage creatures; they may have vicious fights among themselves but will usually not attack their handler.

Husky dogs have a social sense; they form groups based sometimes on a common mother or on a pulling partnership or on a simple friendship. If one of a group gets involved in a fight, the mates jump in to defend him or her. The dogs are loyal as well to the person who takes care of them; this loyalty is returned to the dog in the form of affection and good care. A reasonable driver thinks of his or her dogs before him- or herself; a driver knows each dog by name and by the dog's character. The driver checks the feet of a lame dog or sees to a sore shoulder rubbed by the harness. He or she ensures that each dog gets food (in earlier days, often a one-pound piece of pemmican—a dried food cake—with meat or fish) and that all dogs are tethered to avoid fights. When all the huskies are bedded down, curled into tight balls and secure from the wind, only then does the driver attend to his or her own needs.

A relatively meager ration, one pound of food, actually keeps a dog pulling a sledge for eight to 10 hours, with few rest stops. As each dog can pull about 100 pounds, a 1,000-pound sledge is hauled by a 10-dog team. The huskies are put in a harness, usually a shoulder strap with traces on both sides that go back to the driver. Several dogs may be harnessed together in a line so that the front dog makes a track that the others behind can run in (the dogs like to walk in an established track). Other times each dog has its own traces, all of equal length, so that the team spreads out like a fan in front of the driver. The dogs like speed; when the going is good, the sledge flies like the wind, with each dog pulling hard and the lead dog showing the way and setting the pace. But sometimes, especially if the going is rough, the driver has to urge the dogs on, sometimes getting off the sled to help lead through rough terrain. If problems are not handled, the whole team could deteriorate into a chaos of tangled harnesses and snarling, fighting dogs.

In North America, sledge-pulling dogs have traditionally been called "huskies" or "eskimo dogs." There are different breeds, however. Siberians developed the Samoyed; the Inuit in one part of Alaska bred the malamute. In Greenland and Labrador, the Inuit developed what would become known as the Inuit husky, or Canadian husky. Another husky would be introduced into Alaska as recently as 1911.

The husky dog was the mainstay of the Inuit for many hundreds of years before it was used by European polar explorers. It was 1859 before the Englishman Leopold McClintock used dogs as well as men to pull sledges in his search for Sir John Franklin. Charles Francis Hall, an American, was probably the first non-Inuit to use dog teams as his main method of haulage and travel, in his search for Franklin in 1869. Roald Amundsen used the Siberian Samoyed in his race to the South Pole in 1911.

Without the dogs, travel was slow, dangerous, or impossible. Only the rare, exceptional voyager could transport enough food, fuel, and necessities by manpower to make travel and exploration possible. Although the snowmobile and other vehicles are used today in the polar regions, the dog will remain an essential element in overland polar travel.

Dogs and the sledges that they pulled were instrumental in furthering overland exploration in Antarctica. (*Library of Congress, Prints and Photographs Division [LOT 11453-1, no. 481]*)

This area, the western coast of Antarctica, was at this time almost completely unknown, and Drygalski named it Kaiser Wilhelm II Land. Drygalski and his team of scientists set up observatories on the ice floes, and sledging parties were sent inland to collect scientific data. Drygalski himself ascended in a captive balloon to 1,500 feet and observed the mountains and the glaciers that fed into the West Ice Shelf. At the end of the polar summer, the *Gauss* was freed from 20-foot-thick ice, and the party sailed and steamed back to Cape Town. Although not an especially adventurous expedition, Drygalski summed it up in his book *Southern Ice Continent:* "After a year spent in the same place, we could say that we knew what Nature offered there."

Simultaneously, a Swedish expedition was launched in 1901 led by Otto Nordenskjöld (nephew of Baron [Adolf Erik] Nordenskjöld of the Northeast Passage) aboard the *Antarctica.* The purpose of the exploration was to investigate geological links between the tip of South America and the Antarctic Peninsula. The expedition was plagued with difficulties, and the *Antarctica* eventually sank; trapped for months on a barren island, at one point Nordenskjöld wrote in his journal, later included in his book, *Antarctica:* "It is not easy to reconcile oneself to lying here uselessly and to listen to the howling of the storm, and to know nothing but that our provisions are coming to an end and that our poor dogs are becoming weaker." But in 1904 Nordenskjöld and his men were rescued by an Argentine vessel, and they returned to Sweden with much scientific data, including accurate and extensive maps of the peninsula, and Graham Land in particular.

The most successful of the three 1901 missions was the British expedition headed by Robert Falcon Scott on the *Discovery.* Scott was to follow the path of Ross and carefully explore the region of Victoria Land as a viable entry point for exploration into the interior of the continent. The *Discovery* passed through the ice pack and reached the Ross Ice Shelf early in 1902. Scott reluctantly went aloft in a captive balloon to 800 feet where below he could see his sledging party moving along the top of the shelf, looking for a place to winter. After some further exploration, the *Discovery* steamed west to McMurdo Sound, finding a wintering place on Ross Island. Observatories and monitoring huts were set up, but the crew mainly remained on board, as the anchorage found was most convenient. The winter passed comfortably, despite the total darkness that had descended, bringing with it the moodiness and depression that affects people living in such isolation.

In October 1902—late spring in Antarctica—Scott decided to make a trek to the south; he probably had in mind the possibility of a polar assault (an attempt to reach the North or South Pole), although he did not say so. He took with him Dr. Edward Wilson and Ernest Shackleton, a young, outgoing Anglo-Irishman (who was on the Antarctic expedition not for knowledge but to make some money). Each man had a sledge and a six-dog team. The going was very rough: The team fought through deep snow, rough ice, bouts of scurvy, freezing, snow blindness, and constant hunger. Christmas Day was bleak, but spirits rose when Shackleton produced a Christmas pudding that he had been hiding in a pair of socks. When Scott and the men turned back, they had reached 82°16' S, 200 miles closer to the Pole than any explorer had previously reached. Scott would write in *The Voyage of the "Discovery"*: "[T]he most imaginative cartographer has not dared to cross this limit."

When the three men stumbled back to the base, their provisions had run out, and every dog was dead. Shackleton was on his last legs but had pulled his share up to the final day; he was no longer the money-craving adventurer but rather had fallen victim to the lure of the Antarctic and vowed to return again. Scott returned to England in 1904, to great praise. The research accomplished by the scientific staff was massive and useful to all subsequent exploration.

In 1903, Jean-Baptiste Charcot, a Frenchman, was among those who carried out substantial exploration. Aboard the *Français,* a modest expedition was undertaken to chart the fairly unknown region of the east coast of the Antarctic Peninsula. Charcot overwintered at the Briscoe Islands and went on to explore Alexander Island. On his second voyage (1909), aboard the *Pourquoi-Pas?,* Charcot continued his exploration of the peninsula and discovered Charcot Land (later renamed Charcot Island). Charcot was an exacting and conscientious scientist who provided invaluable accurate maps for later travelers, as well as a wealth of data in the fields of hydrography, geology, zoology, and botany. Also, Charcot was a committed conservationist and warned the whalers, among whom he worked and who assisted him, of the irreversible danger of overhunting. In many ways, Charcot was the model of an enlightened explorer: His interests were entirely scientific; he would have enjoyed being the first to the Pole, but that goal was at the bottom of his priorities.

THE RACE FOR THE POLE

Where Charcot was reserved and quiet in character, in search of knowledge rather than fame, Ernest Shackleton was extroverted and bold and had the conquest of the South Pole as his main motivation for exploration. On his expeditions, however, Shackleton's bravery and determination were to far outweigh these other traits. Shackleton, recovered from illness resulting from the *Discovery* mission, prepared in 1907 for an assault on the Pole. After some frantic fund-raising and some last-minute organization of supplies and crew, the *Nimrod* left England and arrived at the Bay of Whales (east of the Ross Ice Shelf) in January 1908. The inlet there was closed, so Shackleton was forced to go to the west side of the shelf, Ross Island in McMurdo Sound. This was Scott's territory, by rights of discovery, and Scott had asked Shackleton not to begin his polar quest from there. For Shackleton, however, there was no alternative. The *Nimrod* retreated to New Zealand for the winter, and the Shackleton party planned three explorations: Two would explore the mountains and the Ross Ice Shelf; the third, under Shackleton, would make an assault on the Pole. Four men left McMurdo Sound for the Pole on October 29, 1908: Frank Wild, J. B. Adams, Dr. Eric Marshall, and Shackleton. The few dogs they had brought were left behind (along with a motor car); instead, they decided to use man-hauled sledges and Siberian ponies. It was a month before the explorers found a good route to the Pole, and by that time much of the food had been eaten. The four ponies of the expedition were at this point in very bad physical condition. Not only were they suffering from exertion and cold; they had also developed painful snow blindness. One by one the first three ponies were killed and eaten, and stashes of 80 to 100 pounds of the meat from each were buried in the ice, to be saved for the return trip. Only one pony remained: Socks. He was desperately needed to replenish the almost exhausted food supplies. On December 2, Socks fell into a crevasse and was lost, and the men gladly ate the food that had been reserved for the ponies. By January 1909, the party had reached 88°23' S, by far a new record and less than 100 miles from the Pole. Shackleton knew that to go one step further, however, would eliminate any hope of return; he was not prepared to press on to the Pole and die there. So the explorers returned, fighting through the terrible blizzards that had accompanied them throughout the expedition. The return was easier, if only because of the lightness of the sledges, by now almost devoid of food and fuel. The crew who had remained to explore out of the base camp had produced significant scientific data; the expedition was deemed a success by the scientific community.

In 1910, Roald Amundsen and Robert Scott were separately sailing to Antarctica with a common goal: to reach the South Pole. For Scott, the attempt was to be a scientific endeavor; his contingent of scientists in all fields and the huge amounts of scientific apparatus aboard was evidence that the conquest of the Pole was not his only objective. On his ship, the *Terra Nova*, were 65 men, 33 dogs, 19 Siberian ponies, three motorized sledges, and mountains of scientific equipment. His plans called for a full agenda of experiments and observations, and a number of interior and coastal excursions. Furthermore, even after he received word that his Norwegian counterpart was heading south, he did not alter his schedule. He was not to be pushed into a "race" with Amundsen or a competition for the Pole at the sacrifice of his intended work.

In contrast, Amundsen was unabashedly clear about his purposes. In 1910, he had just set out for the North Pole when he heard of Peary's success there. He immediately headed to Antarctica to be the first to reach the South Pole, instead, since the other was denied him. Amundsen, who had seen service in Antarctica, did not consider the South Pole to be the property of any one person or nation,

although it is clear he knew of Scott's intended bid for that last great geographical prize. On Amundsen's *Fram* there was no wealth of scientific instruments. Where instruments and motor sledges might have been was a special "air-conditioned" deck built especially for dogs to keep them cool and in tip-top condition. The *Fram* carried not 33 but 97 dogs, handpicked and the best that money could buy. And there were only 19 men, specially chosen as well, who included the best dog team drivers Amundsen could find.

Amundsen picked his base location well, based on careful research into the experiences of earlier explorers and his knowledge of polar geology. He chose the Bay of Whales area because he knew that the gently sloping ice there was land fast and therefore stable. It was also 60 miles closer to the Pole than McMurdo Sound, where Scott went. (In the end, 60 miles might have made an enormous difference to Scott.) Furthermore, the weather was much more moderate at the Bay of Whales.

By February 1911, Amundsen and his men had constructed Framheim (home of the *Fram*), a 26-by-13-foot hut, well insulated, with a bunk and stool for each man, officers and crew alike. Two stoves kept the interior warm and cozy, and there was an abundance of food. From Amundsen's base a good route to the Pole was available, and the men immediately began to place food depots along the intended route to the Pole: at 80° S two tons of supplies, at 81° S and 82° S lesser amounts. Each depot was marked with a snow beacon. (A snow beacon is a trail marker made of shiny material that in sunlight shines like a bright light, visible for miles; in a snowstorm, it is a black spot against the whiteness of the snow.) These markers were also placed every five or six miles to identify the trail. Winter was fast approaching; by the time the last depot was established, the temperature had dropped to

−52° Fahrenheit and the sun had sunk, not to be seen again for four months. It was time to retire to the Framheim and prepare for the attempt when spring came.

What lay ahead of Amundsen? First there was the barrier: the Ross Ice Shelf. After 400 miles of that, they would reach "land," if rock covered by two miles of ice cap can be called land. Then there were the glaciers leading to the mountains (Queen Maud Range), some of which rose to 16,000 feet. Finally, there would be the central frozen plateau and whatever unforeseen and unknown dangers might lie in wait. All in all, 870 miles of terrain, never seen by human eye, lay between Amundsen and the Pole.

Undaunted, and eager to begin, the party left Framheim in early September, but soon returned when the temperature dropped to −72° Fahrenheit, which was much too cold for the dogs. Five weeks later, spring had really come, and on October 19, 1911, five men began the quest: Helmen Hanssen (an outstanding dog driver), Oscar Wisting, Sverre Hassel, Olav Bjaaland, and Roald, as Amund-

sen was called by all the men. From the start, despite some days of bad weather, it was clear, that this was to be an easy trek. The sledges were lightly loaded because the depots of food awaited them; the dogs pulled with gusto, and the drivers often held onto the sledges and were pulled along swiftly on skis. The pressure ridges of the Arctic Ocean were not present in the South, either, so there was no need to hack and cut through 20-foot piles of broken ice.

As the limit of Ross Ice Shelf was reached, the surface altered slightly, and the men realized they were over land (however far below it was), and the slope became slightly uphill as the mountains that lay between the ice shelf and the central plateau loomed into sight. The weather held mostly favorable, and the temperature never dropped below −30° Fahrenheit. The way now was marked by crevasses, some yawning open but mostly hidden by innocent-looking drifts of snow or barely visible little domes of snow, hollow underneath and deadly to dogs and men. Many of the crevasses were so deep that the men could not

Roald Amundsen used dogs and sledges similar to the ones shown here in the race to the South Pole in late 1911. *(Library of Congress, Prints and Photographs Division [LOT 11453-1, no. 48])*

see the bottom. Higher and higher the party ascended up the Queen Maud Mountains; this was the most difficult part of the journey. Amundsen, reaching a pass between mountains, spotted a glacier that led to the central plateau, and he realized that this was his avenue through the mountains to the plateau on top. Just before leaving the mountain range, there was a brief but sad pause. Here, no longer needed for transport but needed for food, 24 of the dogs were to be slaughtered and fed to their surviving mates. Any man who had depended on these faithful creatures for his survival could face such a moment only with extreme regret and sadness. As the first shots were fired, Amundsen would later write, he remained in the tent stirring a big cooking pot with a big spoon, making as much noise as possible, drowning out the sounds. Amundsen also wrote that his men named the site "Butcher's Shop."

When the high plateau was reached, victory was just a matter of careful navigation; a few days of bad weather were merely a minor distraction and a chance to get some extra rest. On December 8, the party passed Shackleton's "farthest-south" point, and a Norwegian flag was put on the front of the lead sledge. On December 14, 1911, Hanssen, driving the lead sledge, asked Amundsen to walk in front because "the dogs run better with someone in front of them." Thus, when at 3:00 P.M. that day, the Pole was reached, the men ensured that Amundsen was the first to be there. Amundsen would describe it in his book *The South Pole:*

> After we had halted we collected and congratulated each other . . . After this we proceeded to the greatest and most solemn act of the whole journey—the planting of our [Norwegian] flag. . . . I had determined that the act of planting it—the historic event—

> should be equally divided among us all. It was not for one man to do this; it was for *all* who had staked their lives in the struggle, and held together through thick and thin . . . Five weather-beaten, frost-bitten fists they were that grasped the pole, raised the waving flag in the air and planted it as the first at the geographical South Pole.

The return to base was almost ridiculously easy. The party followed the trail, marked with snow beacons and flags, with ease. The depots were still stocked with food and fuel; the men were annoyed that Amundsen limited their speed to 17 1/2 miles per day (later increased to 20 miles and more). The dogs were eating pemmican and biscuits now and even chocolate; they were gaining weight. Never has such an expedition been carried out with such ease. Amundsen called it luck; others called it a masterful job of organization, preparation, and discipline. A short time later, the *Fram* was on its way back to tumultuous acclaim in Norway. At the South Pole, a tent had been erected by the departing Norwegians; a flag was tied to the top, and inside there were two letters: One was to King Haakon VII of Norway, and the other was addressed to Captain Robert Falcon Scott.

SCOTT'S FINAL WEEKS

On February 2, 1912, as the *Fram* was beginning its victory voyage home, Scott was writing an entry in his journal: "Friday, February 2nd, three out of five of us injured. We shall be lucky if we get through." Huddled in the tent, low on food and lower on fuel, pinned down by bad weather and physically broken down, Scott must have realized that about 700 miles lay between the worn-out explorers and base camp, 700 miles that they could not possibly survive.

On January 17, Scott, along with the final team, Edward Wilson, Edgar Evans, L. E. G.

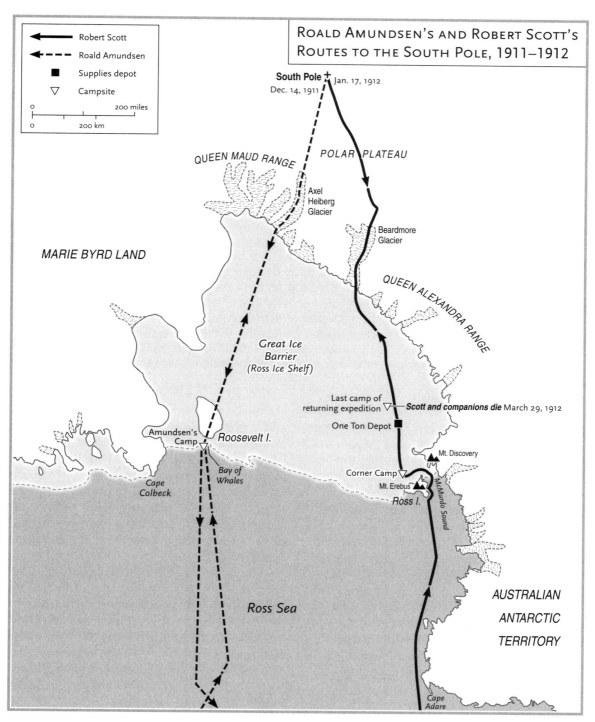

ROALD AMUNDSEN'S AND ROBERT SCOTT'S
ROUTES TO THE SOUTH POLE, 1911–1912

Robert Scott
Roald Amundsen
Supplies depot
Campsite

0   200 miles
0   200 km

South Pole ✝ Jan. 17, 1912
Dec. 14, 1911

QUEEN MAUD RANGE   POLAR PLATEAU

Axel
Heiberg
Glacier

Beardmore
Glacier

MARIE BYRD LAND

QUEEN ALEXANDRA RANGE

Great Ice
Barrier
(Ross Ice Shelf)

Last camp of
returning expedition ▽ *Scott and companions die* March 29, 1912

One Ton Depot ■

Amundsen's
Camp ▽   Roosevelt I.

*Bay of
Whales*

Corner Camp ▽

Mt. Discovery ▲

Cape
Colbeck

Mt. Erebus ▲

Ross I.

McMurdo Sound

Ross Sea

AUSTRALIAN

ANTARCTIC

TERRITORY

Cape
Adare

Robert Scott's Fatal Decision ⟋

Robert Scott, following British tradition, did not believe in using dogs. It is puzzling that in Arctic exploration the British had never believed in the efficacy of dogs for hauling supplies; expeditions, one after another, failed because men could not haul enough supplies to survive. Scott had not the slightest expertise in the use of dogs. For his 1910 polar expedition, on which he finally planned to use them for haulage, he did not know how to feed them, take care of them, or drive them. Furthermore, unlike Amundsen, he did not bother to find someone who could. It is foolish for an inexperienced person to attempt to deal with a pack of half-wild creatures. Small wonder that Scott wrote in his journal in March 1911: "Bit by bit, I am losing all faith in them." In fact, he had already decided against using dogs to haul food and fuel in his attempt on the South Pole before he arrived at McMurdo Sound Bay. He brought with him only 33 dogs to be used in stocking the depots (caches of food and fuel to be used on the return). Hauling to the Pole and back was to be done by manpower, Siberian ponies, and three motorized sledges. The dog teams were inadequate to stock depots beyond 79° S. There were too few of them, and this part of the preparation had been disorganized and neglected. After the too few and inadequate depots were stocked, the dogs were driven back to the base camp. The expedition set off with the Siberian ponies, who soon died from cold or were shot. None of the three motorized sledges got any further than 50 miles from base camp.

Oates, and Henry R. Bowers, had reached the South Pole to find the debris and evidence of Amundsen's earlier arrival there. The five explorers began the 900-mile trek back to base with disappointment, despair, and apprehension. Nothing went well for the explorers. Supplies of food and fuel at the depots were short, and lower rations per day were required; the weather had turned bitterly cold and stormy. Evans was the first to break down; his hands were so badly frozen that they were useless, and he possibly was suffering from a concussion from a fall. He was, as well, "losing heart." On February 17, he died quietly in the tent. Bowers and Wilson were suffering from snow blindness. Oates was in a most desperate condition: His feet had been frozen for weeks; now, one foot had turned completely black,

and it was a miracle that he could walk. Scott's journal for March 16 or 17 (he was not sure what day it was) includes: "Poor Titus Oates said he couldn't go on; he proposed we should leave him in his sleeping bag. That we could not do." The next morning Oates said, "I am just going outside and may be some time." He went out into the blizzard and was not seen again.

The relentless blizzard with its high gale winds continued throughout March. The weather was abnormally severe for summer in Antarctica. The temperature hovered around −40° Fahrenheit, but it was the everlasting wind that kept the men in the tent. On March 20, the three remaining explorers were just 11 miles from a one-ton depot where there were abundant supplies. In the

Scott was opposed to using dogs for several reasons. For one, he preferred man-hauling because "No journey made with dogs can approach the sublimity of a party of men," wrote Scott in his journal in March 1911. He also opposed using dogs on humanitarian grounds because the accepted practice was that they were first to provide transport and when supplies ran low the first to provide food. Amundsen reasoned, however, in his autobiography that as there were 50 pounds of edible meat in a husky carcass, that was 50 pounds of meat that did not need to be hauled: "I intended to kill each dog as its usefulness for pulling supplies diminished and its usefulness as food increased." Scott would have found this attitude appalling and unacceptable. Yet somehow these scruples did not seem to apply to the use and execution of ponies: In early December 1911, after 14 ponies had died from the cold, the last five were shot; there is no indication as to what was done with the carcasses. The 33 dogs were used to pull sledges part way but went back to the base camp as planned.

Scott had not paid sufficient attention to the necessity of transporting enough food and supplies to last the duration of his attempt at reaching the Pole. Even in the preparation phase of operations, he was unable to set up depots to ensure his return. No supplies were cached beyond 79° S, whereas Amundsen had depots at 80°, 81°, and 82° S. Lack of cached food and fuel for the return was directly responsible for the plight of Scott and his death 11 miles from a depot.

tent was fuel enough for two cups of tea per man, but no food. Survival time outside was perhaps 100 yards, because of the wind. The 11 miles might just as well have been 100. It was at this time that Scott wrote messages to the families of his final companions, attesting to their strength and honorable conduct and their bravery. On March 29, Scott wrote in his journal:

Great God! This is an awful place and terrible enough for us to have laboured without the reward of priority. . . . We took risks, we knew we took them. . . . Had we lived, I should have had a tale to tell of the hardihood, endurance, and courage of my companions. These rough notes and our dead bodies must tell the tale.

On March 31, Scott's final message, "to the public" ended this way: "It seems a pity but I do not think I can write more. R. Scott Last entry. For God's sake look after our people."

The search party that came in November 1912 found the three men peacefully lying in the tent, covered by snow. The tent was lowered over them and a cairn was built above. It has been supposed that the cairn is now at least 50 feet under the snow and 20 miles nearer the edge of the Ross Ice Shelf.

Yet the conquest of the South Pole was not the end of Antarctica exploration; rather, it was the beginning. Perhaps it was a good thing to get that distracting, illusory goal over and done with. There was so much to learn, to find, to profit in knowledge from the southern continent. The real work of exploration lay ahead.

8

THE ARCTIC AFTER PEARY

 The Arctic explorer Wally Herbert, in his 1989 biography of Robert Peary, *Noose of Laurels,* addresses the question of Peary's disputed reaching the North Pole. It is clear that Herbert has great admiration for Peary and his many achievements but cannot accept his claim to be first to discover the North Pole. He describes Peary's hearing the news that Dr. Frederick Cook had reached the Pole in August 1909 and how the bitterness began to form within him that became a "cancer in his soul which by slow degrees destroyed him." By Herbert's calculations, Peary ended up 50 miles west and one degree south of the Pole. Even so, like many other 20th-century Arctic explorers who from their own experience understood the horrific struggle Peary underwent in his whole career, Herbert believes that Peary should be given the Pole. What is an error of 50 miles, compared to the thousands achieved in pain and single-minded determination?

Before Peary's claim there had been a fury of Arctic activity, almost all directed at being the first to the Pole. Travel writer Deanna Swaney in *The Arctic,* counts 17 expeditions

Many expeditions attempted to reach the North Pole between 1895 and 1915. The mission pictured here at 82° north latitude failed in their attempt. *(Library of Congress, Prints and Photographs Division [LC-USZ62-122849])*

that attempted to reach the North Pole from 1895 (the *Fram* exploration) to 1915. Countries represented were Italy, Germany, Norway, Russia, Sweden, and the United States. Going further back, many of the search expeditions for John Franklin had a polar search as their covert purpose. The quest for the Pole had been a real impetus for Arctic exploration. After Peary, the nature of Arctic exploration had to change.

STEFANSSON AND SVERDRUP

With the storm clouds of World War I lowering upon the Western world, there was a pause in such unessential activity as exploring the wasteland of the Arctic. There were, however, two explorers who had never been particularly interested in being the first to reach the Pole, they continued to do as they had always done: to add to the maps the new lands and waters that they saw and explored. The first of these two men was the Canadian-born Vilhjalmur Stefansson, "the Champion of the North." He had spent his lifetime in the Canadian far north and had added about 100,000 square miles to the map. In addition, to his travels and discoveries, he contributed a wealth of information to the world about the lives and customs of the Inuit people. Stefansson was probably the first non-native to understand the concept of living off the land in the Arctic, using the Inuit ways of being in touch with the harsh arctic natural world and taking advantage of what it offered for survival. As Stefansson expressed in his book, *Friendly Arctic*, "I feel like mentioning that I cannot understand the psychology of northern travellers who employ Eskimos and Indians to do their hunting for them. I would as soon think of engaging a valet to play my golf or of going to the theatre by proxy."

When Stefansson's ship, the *Karluk*, was lost off the shore of Alaska in 1913, Stefansson

Mukpi, a little Inuit girl, was the youngest survivor of the *Karluk* crew when the ship became lost near Alaska in 1913. *(Library of Congress, Prints and Photographs Division [LOT 11453-3, no. 16])*

with two seamen walked from Barrow Point to Banks Island, a distance of 700 miles across the most barren and lifeless part of the Arctic Ocean, the Beaufort Sea. While walking, Stefansson mapped the position of the continental shelf off the coast of Alaska. When Banks Island was reached Stefansson had charted the whole western coast. Along the way, Stefansson was marooned on an ice floe, from which he collected meteorological data, took line soundings, and kept records

An Unsung Hero

Of all the Arctic expeditions that immediately followed Peary's conquest of the North Pole, the saddest and most tragic was that of Georgiy Yakovlevich Sedov. Sedov, born into poverty, did not attend school until he was 15; he nevertheless got into St. Petersburg Naval College, and while there became interested in the Northeast Passage, which he foresaw as critically important to the future development of Siberia. After graduation, with very little financial support, he managed to complete a survey of the north Siberian tundra. In 1909, with a ship, he explored the Siberian coastline and produced a report that contained important and new data on navigation, tides, rivers flowing into the Arctic, and other information pertinent to the Northeast Passage. The reward for his efforts was an appointment to the Imperial Russian Navy as an officer, an incredible achievement as he had no money, influence, or title, the usual prerequisites. Not content to rest on his newfound laurel, Sedov petitioned the government in 1912 for money to explore Franz Josef Land on the way to an expedition to the North Pole.

Sedov was turned down—he had neither the reputation nor the influence to sway the naval authorities—so Sedov turned to the public and managed to raise enough money to buy a worn-out ship, the *Foka,* and have a bit left over for provisions. The merchants of Arkhangelsk, a city and seaport on Russia's north coast, took advantage of Sedov; all of his provisions were of inferior quality, and no attention was paid to scurvy-preventive foods. From the beginning the expedition was spoken of as a suicide mission. Red tape plagued Sedov. Regulations about the *Foka*'s waterline caused a ban on the ship's leaving harbor. Sedov swept deck cargo off into the harbor water, careless of what vital cargo he was destroying.

Finally, in late September 1912, the *Foka* cleared the harbor of Arkhangelsk, but because of the delays, the expedition was unable to make Franz Josef Land and was frozen in at Novaya Zemlya. A year was spent marking time, using up paltry and insufficient food and fuel supplies. Pleas to the Russian navy for

of water and air temperatures and patterns of ice deterioration and ice floe melt. Stefansson later described the entire excursion as a "picnic." Stefansson retired from active exploration in 1919, after sledging more than 5,000 miles through the Canadian archipelago and the far Arctic. His point farthest north was 80°, where he discovered (among many other places) Meighen Island. He maintained

that he never had an interest in going to the North Pole: that, he said, was for tourists, not scientists.

The second explorer, Otto Sverdrup, from Norway, finished his Arctic work a decade before World War I began. Sverdrup, like Stefansson, was not interested in reaching the North Pole; Peary, however, thought he was and warned him to keep away from his terri-

additional food and fuel went unanswered. One year later, in September 1913, the officers of the *Foka* pleaded with Sedov to abort the mission and return home. Sedov wrote in his journal: "Today the officers made me a fine gift: through the officer of the watch, they proposed turning back. At first this really amazed me, then it pained me, because I had to refuse them."

The *Foka*, finally free, reached Northbrook Island, Franz Josef Land, on September 16, 1913. By this time, the fuel was gone, and the crew was burning blubber, ropes, and old sails to keep the engine going. Near Cape Flora, on Northbrook Island, the party found a small abandoned store of coal: With this bonanza they were able to steam to Hooker Island, a little further north in the Franz Josef Archipelago. At this point they were again locked into the ice. Now down to piles of coal dust, the men began to burn parts of the inside of the ship. By Christmas 1913, all but three of the men were disabled with scurvy. Sedov wrote on January 2, 1914, in his journal: "Legs completely paralysed." The worse conditions on the ship got, the more manically determined Sedov was to "carry out his duty." Sadly, he did not realize that he had no "duty." The Russian admiralty had no concern for him and had ignored his requests for aid.

On February 15, 1914, still incapacitated by scurvy, Sedov left for the North Pole with two sailors, three sledges, and 24 dogs. If there ever was a suicide mission, this was it. The temperature stood at −104° Fahrenheit and the condition of the ice was terrible. After one week, Sedov was unable to walk. At his companions' pleas to turn back, he would only smile. He went on, for two more days, "doing his duty," and then died on February 24, 1914. After waiting out a three-day blizzard, the two sailors buried Sedov in the snow along with the flag he intended to deposit at the Pole. The sailors struggled back to the *Foka* (they had not gotten very far), and the *Foka* struggled back to Arkhangelsk in September 1914 by burning everything in the ship but the hull and the mast.

There was no welcome party waiting for the *Foka;* Russia was involved in World War I. Sedov's findings, and his journal were sent to the archives. It was 45 years after his death when they were opened and first read.

tory. Peary also warned Sverdrup that Greenland was off limits to him. Peary's possessive attitude is difficult to understand, since Sverdrup had crossed the Greenland ice cap with Nansen in 1888. Peary's worries about Sverdrup's plans were groundless. Sverdrup was first of all a seaman, having the reputation of being an outstanding navigator and a highly skillful ship captain. His interest was in discovery of new lands and the charting of unknown areas of the Canadian archipelago. Sverdrup had been the captain of the *Fram* on the 1893 voyage with Fridtjof Nansen. When Nansen left the *Fram* for his attempt on foot for the North Pole, Sverdrup had guided the *Fram* and crew through very difficult conditions, to safety at Spitsbergen. Later, after being driven away from Greenland

Vilhjalmur Stefansson learned much from the Inuit people. In this photograph, eight Inuit and one Caucasian man display dog sleds that they built in Alaska for the Stefansson expedition's use. *(Library of Congress, Prints and Photographs Division [LC-USZ62-103517])*

by Peary, he extensively explored the regions to the west. In 1899, with great accuracy, he charted the west coast of Ellesmere Island and discovered the islands of Axel Heiberg, Amund Ringnes, and Ellef Ringnes. Sverdrup succeeded in adding a huge area of the Arctic to the map—many thousands of square miles—and his voyages are perhaps less publicized than other explorers because they were carried out with no disasters or loss of life. He returned home to retirement in Norway; the one disappointment in his career was that he and his master, Nansen, had not gone exploring at the South Pole.

NEW EQUIPMENT, NEW GOALS

Interest in the Arctic was resumed after the ending of the war in 1918, and now great technological developments were to influence the methods and capabilities of northern exploration. The ships themselves were vastly different in the 1920s and 1930s; huge icebreakers with powerful diesel engines made the expeditions' ships less vulnerable to the ice packs. The new ships, giants compared to the old sailing vessels, had increased capacity for storage of machinery, fresh food, and supplies and comfortable quarters for the crew. In every way the expeditions were less at the mercy of the unpredictable weather. Some ships carried their own airplanes; every exploring ship had a radio, which connected it to the outside world. In an emergency, airplanes could be sent to a vessel in trouble. With reliable charts and maps and improved navigation aids, such as radar, there was little chance of a ship going off course or missing its destination.

The war had brought about great improvements in the design and efficiency of the airplane. Engines were larger and more reliable, and there were many men now skilled in aircraft maintenance. The range of the airplane was much greater than before; long flights could be made without refueling, eliminating the danger of landings and takeoffs under dangerous conditions. Planes were outfitted with skis, for operation in snow, and by 1925, the "flying boat" was in use, capable of landing on water or even smooth ice.

Land vehicles had been developed that were reliable and effective in cold weather conditions. Some of the earlier motorized sledges had traveled 50 feet in the antarctic cold and then stopped, frozen up; one model was stymied by three inches of snow. Now tank-like Sno-Cats and snowmobiles could pull trailers of fuel and were capable of reaching the North Pole from Greenland with fuel to spare.

The aims of polar exploration also had changed. Since the Pole had been achieved by Peary, there were attempts to duplicate the feat in other ways: over the Pole in the air, and under the Pole, beneath the ice. Whereas, in Antarctica in the 20th century, much of the exploration had specific scientific goals, in the Arctic this objective was true only of some of the time and much of the post–World War I Arctic exploration was carried out by adventurers rather than scientists or explorers.

Also, the war alerted many countries, particularly the Soviet Union and the United States, to the potential strategic importance of the Arctic; therefore, some of the polar activity had a nationalistic motivation to it. The early exploration of the Greenland ice cap in 1912 by native Greenlander Knud Rasmussen and Peter Freuchen, a Dane, was a scientific mission, as well as a demonstration of Danish sovereignty of Greenland. (Rasmussen was passionately opposed to the presence of American whalers in Greenland.) German Alfred Wegener had crossed the Greenland ice cap in 1913 (using ponies for haulage); in 1930, he returned with a party and established a scientific station in the highlands of the ice cap, bringing with him 10 tons of scientific equipment. The British also were active at this time in Greenland: Gino Watkins was the leader of

As Arctic expedition grew more sophisticated, airplanes became quite useful. Charles Lindbergh (standing, center); Anne Morrow Lindbergh, his wife (in plane); and some navy radio operators test equipment before the Lindberghs begin a 7,100-mile vacation flight. *(Library of Congress, Prints and Photographs Division [LC-USZ62-97591])*

an expedition that established a meteorological observatory in the ice cap. Notable in this expedition was the attempt of Augustine Courtauld to winter in solitude in a hut on the ice cap. At the last moment Courtauld was rescued from death by starvation, cold, and a blocked ventilator.

AIRCRAFT IN THE ARCTIC

Practically all exploration in the Arctic (and the Antarctic) after World War I was carried out or supported by aircraft, small single- or twin-engine planes that were equipped with wheels or skis for landing, or less frequently, pontoons for landing in water. Also developed after the war was the so-called flying boat. It had a wide, bulging fuselage so that it could land and then float right on the water. The flying boat could also land on frozen water or land if the runway was smooth enough. Finally there was the airship, or dirigible, inspired by the hot-air balloon but filled with gas and driven by a small propeller, at fairly low speed.

There is no question that polar exploration, with the aid of reliable aircraft, was

Richard Byrd tests his sextant, a navigational instrument used to measure distances between celestial bodies, before his flight to the North Pole, as an unidentified man looks on. *(Library of Congress, Prints and Photographs Division [LC-USZ62-20260])*

These airplanes, frozen in ice, were piloted by Roald Amundsen and Lincoln Ellsworth in a failed attempt to fly over the North Pole in 1925. *(Library of Congress, Prints and Photographs Division [LC-USZ62-22757])*

unlike pre-20th-century exploration. Flying over the North Pole today is the same as flying from Paris to London, but it was not always so simple. The first Arctic flights, made by the Russians in Siberia in 1914, were dangerous in that any serious mechanical breakdown would probably result in death. The pioneers in Arctic flight were mostly men who had the explorer spirit and mentality anyhow; they merely took advantage of a technological innovation to do better what they had already intended to do. Great credit must be given to Richard Byrd, the U.S. naval officer, for his successful efforts to make flying an essential part of polar exploration. Byrd's extensive fieldwork in the Arctic and Antarctica and his skill in surface travel and survival were matched by his scientific interests and his geographical interests and achievements. Byrd was able to turn his fanatic love of the airplane—and his belief in it as a powerful tool of exploration—into a new status for aircraft as a permanent factor in the years to come. Byrd's claim to have flown over the North Pole on May 9, 1926, has been questioned over the years, but his feat has not really been discredited. The prevailing opinion by historians is that the 1926 polar flight

Roald Amundsen (probably left, facing camera) and Richard Byrd (probably right, facing camera) stand on the deck of the *Chantier* after Byrd's successful flight over the North Pole on May 9, 1926. *(Library of Congress, Prints and Photographs Division [LC-USZ62-107010])*

Umberto Nobile, holding a small dog in Nome, Alaska, designed and built the airship *Norge*. *(Library of Congress, Prints and Photographs Division [LC-USZ62-100819])*

In 1925, Amundsen joined up with Lincoln Ellsworth, a wealthy U.S. adventurer, who would become a worthy and resourceful explorer; he was later decorated for bravery by King Haakon VII of Norway. The expedition was composed of two flying boats, one of which had to land because of engine trouble, and the second was destroyed when it came to the aid of the first. Almost miraculously, both crews were able to fly back to Spitsbergen in the crippled plane, where they were rescued by a sealing boat. Amundsen went on to successfully fly over the North Pole in 1926, this time with Ellsworth in the airship *Norge*,

In 1926, Umberto Nobile, accompanied by Lincoln Ellsworth and Roald Amundsen, piloted his airship *Norge* over the North Pole. Here Nobile walks along the narrow catwalk during the flight. *(Library of Congress, Prints and Photographs Division [LOT 4501])*

was one of the greatest moments in aviation history.

Roald Amundsen, who had shown his mastery of polar exploration using traditional technology, developed a strong interest in aerial exploration by 1909. After he reached the South Pole in 1911, he undertook some scientific work aboard his ship, *Maud,* in the Arctic. Amundsen, who had purchased an airplane in 1914, abandoned the *Maud* expedition and made plans to reach the North Pole by air, a feat not yet accomplished. A proposed attempt in 1923 was abandoned at the last minute because the airplane was not adequate.

The *Chelyuskin* vs. the Northeast Passage

When Premier Joseph Stalin came to power in the Soviet Union in 1929, he was impatient with the delays that had kept the Northeast Passage from developing into the valuable cargo and passenger route it had promised to be. So he set up an organization called the Central Administration of the Northern Sea Route, whose job was to get ships running regularly along the Arctic Ocean from western Russia to the Bering Strait. He appointed the distinguished geophysicist and Arctic veteran Otto Yulevich Schmidt as the head of the project, and Schmidt went into action immediately. By 1932, he had readied the icebreaker *Sibiriakov,* with Vladimir Voronin as captain, for a voyage through the passage. Although the ship broke down a number of times, the voyage was successful: In 65 days, the *Sibiriakov* had traveled from Arkhangelsk to the Pacific Ocean, the first vessel ever to accomplish a passage of the northern sea route without wintering along the way.

Flushed with the success of this first attempt, Schmidt prepared a second vessel, the *Chelyuskin,* by adapting it with a powerful 2,500-horsepower engine, special frame, and reinforcements, and extra steel plates on the bow and forward bulkhead. Its construction would allow it to function as a semi-icebreaker. Confident that the ship would be able to plow through the ice of the Arctic Ocean, Schmidt loaded it up and departed in August 1933 with 100 passengers and heavy cargo bound for Wrangel Island.

By the time the ship reached Cape Chelyuskin (after which it was named), Captain Voronin realized that his vessel was not performing up to expectations and that conditions were worsening rapidly as the summer was drawing to a close. Schmidt considered turning back but decided to plow on through the ever-thickening ice. By mid-September, the *Chelyuskin* was picking its way through narrow leads of water, twisting and turning to avoid the big floes, heading ever eastward. Then, in the East Siberian Sea, 200 miles from the Bering Strait, the ship could move no more. Back and forth the ship drifted, frozen solidly in the pack ice, its powerful engine unable to free it. Suddenly, the ice began to drift steadily to the southeast, and on November 3, the ice pack, with the *Chelyuskin* in it, moved into the Bering Strait. By radio, the captain heard that 12 miles ahead was open water. In a matter of minutes, the *Chelyuskin* would be in the Pacific Ocean free to steam south. Then, without warning, the drift reversed itself and with incredible speed, swept ice and ship to the north, in the grip of a powerful current. After weeks of drifting to the north and northwest, Schmidt realized the ship was in "ancient" ice, meaning the main polar pack. The ship would never be free. With five crew members, he began in secret to prepare to abandon ship.

The end came on February 13, 1934, when a mountain of ice gashed a 40-foot-long hole in the side of the ship, flooding the engine and boiler rooms with

Arctic water. The ship's helmsman, Mikhail Gavrilovich Markov, described what followed in *The Voyage of the Chelyuskin*: "Then the *Chelyuskin*'s bow began to go down rapidly and the last command rang out—'All on the ice! Leave the ship!' The gangway twisted and fell." The last men aboard jumped onto the ice and within minutes the ship sank beneath the sea. The crew and passengers now settled down to make what they named "camp Schmidt" on the ice floes.

These pioneers did not have radios to send messages nor airplanes to come immediately to the rescue, nevertheless, by April 13, 92 men, 10 women, and two infants were airlifted to safety—not a single life lost. The sinking of the *Chelyuskin* did not dampen determination to open the Northeast Passage; rather it served to bring about more powerful icebreakers and a greater resolve to make the passage a viable and profitable sea route.

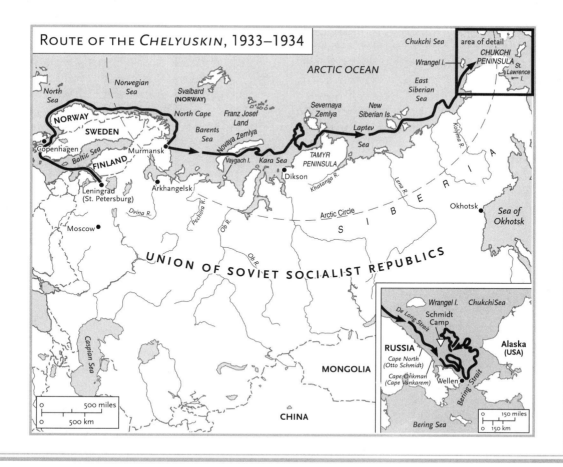

ROUTE OF THE *CHELYUSKIN*, 1933–1934

designed and piloted by Italian aeronautical engineer Umberto Nobile. After dropping the Norwegian, American, and Italian flags to the ice, the *Norge* continued on to Nome, Alaska; a trip of 3,000 miles had been accomplished in 72 hours and the first trans-Arctic flight had been made—from Spitsbergen to Alaska.

Soon after the successful flight of the *Norge*, Nobile designed and built a new and improved airship, the *Italia*. On May 23, 1928, Nobile left to explore, by air, the area north of Greenland and then to proceed, by a new route, to the North Pole. In Nobile's book *My Polar Flight*, he describes the terror of the mysterious malfunction that brought the *Italia*, lower and lower, to the jagged chaos of waiting ice. He later tells of the misunderstanding that caused him to be rescued before the rest of the surviving crew (his being rescued first was comparable to a captain being the first to leave his sinking ship—dishonorable). Humiliation and scorn dogged Nobile for the rest of his life over this affair. One result of the worldwide publicity of the disaster was the lessening of confidence in the airship as an aircraft of exploration.

In 1937, the Russians established a scientific station on the ice near the North Pole, under the command of Ivan Papanin. The many tons of equipment and supplies were carried to the ice floe by four airplanes. The program to be carried out was ambitious: magnetic and meteorological observations and biological and physical analyses of the sea. Water depth was to be measured all along the path of drift. The living quarters were designed using new materials and ideas; For instance, the floor of the collapsible house was made from air-filled cushions and the entire interior was lined with reindeer fur. The floating station drifted from June 1937 to February 1938, and the party was picked up by an icebreaker just off the eastern coast of Greenland. Papanin and his three companions were all in good shape, and an enormous amount of scientific data had been recorded.

THE POLE FROM BENEATH

One of the most colorful explorers of the 20th century was an Australian named Herbert Wilkins: He taught himself about everything his eclectic mind took an interest in. He learned electrical engineering and cartography, taught himself how to fly, and became an expert photographer. Somehow he also managed to join up with Vilhjalmur Stefansson and explored some islands in the northwest Canadian archipelago. Intrigued by the Arctic, by 1926, he made a number of scouting flights over the Beaufort Sea. He was successful, in 1928, in being the first aviator to pilot a plane across the Arctic from Alaska to Spitsbergen. Wilkins also has the distinction of being the first explorer to attempt to reach the North Pole under the ice. He leased a submarine (the O-12) from the U.S. Navy for $1 and with his engineering knowledge, refurbished it and rechristened it the *Nautilus*. Wilkins's partner in this endeavor was Ellsworth, who could always be counted on if there were an adventure in the offing. The attempt to cruise under the Pole in 1931 failed. There were three main requirements for such an exploration, none of which the *Nautilus* met: power, underwater range, and a navigational system.

All of the necessities were dealt with by the construction of the U.S. Navy's submarine, the USS *Nautilus*, 25 years later. In 1958, with William Anderson as commander, the *Nautilus*, with nuclear power, indefinite range, and the new inertial navigational system, submerged in the Chukchi Sea on August 1 and surfaced in the Greenland Sea on August 3, after a two-day uneventful voyage beneath the

Ships such as the U.S. Coast Guard icebreaker *Eastwind* were not as useful as submarines such as the *Nautilus* for Arctic exploration. *(Library of Congress, Prints and Photographs Division [LC-USZ62-97366])*

North Pole. The sister ship of the *Nautilus,* the USS *Skate,* duplicated the feat in the same year, and in 1959 the *Skate* became the first ship to surface at the Pole.

THE POLE CONTINUES TO ATTRACT

Three successful expeditions to the North Pole were carried out between 1968 and 1986. Ralph Plaisted, an insurance salesman from Minnesota, assembled a party of individuals, none of whom had ever been in the Arctic. On his second attempt, using snowmobiles and supported all the way by airplane, Plaisted reached the Pole on April 20, 1968. Those who do not believe that Peary or Cook reached the Pole count instead Plaisted's expedition as the first ever to stand at the true North Pole. It is interesting to note that about one year after Plaisted's victory, the Americans walked on the Moon.

The USS *Nautilus*, a navy submarine, helped advance underwater exploration at the North Pole. It first reached the Pole in August 1958 when it traveled from the Chukchi Sea to the Greenland Sea. *(National Archives, Still Picture Records, NWDNS-80-G-709366)*

Wally Herbert, using dogs as transport, walked across the Arctic Ocean. This British explorer experienced in exploration in Greenland, Antarctica, and the Arctic, left Alaska in 1968 and reached Spitsbergen via the Pole in May 1969, after wintering on the ice. This expedition also had full air support. In 1986, American Will Steger attempted to reach the Pole under the same conditions as those dealt with by Robert Peary. Using dogs and no airplane drops of supplies, he trekked from Ellesmere Island to the Pole, with five companions, including Ann Bancroft, an American and the first woman to reach the Pole. The party and all the dogs were airlifted out at the conclusion of the expedition.

Other expeditions to the Pole occurred in the late 20th century, and others will occur in the future. There will always be a "first" available to those who, with imagination, think of techniques or angles that no one else has tried before. But the real exploration of the Arctic is done. There is not a remote island or portion of the Arctic Ocean that is not on some map, in some photograph. Now, as a tourist, one may stand on the bridge of the *Yamal*, a Russian icebreaker and tourist ship, and drink champagne, as the nuclear-powered engines drive the ship over the North Pole. Perhaps the toast might be to the 400 years of exploration that allowed the present moment. Or perhaps the toast should be to a time, now gone by, when exploration was a deep human expression of individuals' passionate need to find, to understand, and to conquer.

9

ANTARCTICA
AFTER AMUNDSEN

A peculiarity of polar exploration is that before the 20th century, it was ahead of its time, in advance of the technology and scientific knowledge needed to ensure success. For centuries, the British plowed through the Arctic waters in inadequate ships, without maps and charts, without accurate methods of navigation, and without knowledge of polar meteorology, geography, or hydrography. Other examples abound of intrepid explorers facing the terrible rigors of the North and South Polar Regions without a chance of success, given the state of knowledge and equipment that existed at the time. Perhaps it is the quintessential nature of the spirit of exploration to challenge before success is guaranteed, before the trail is broken. Robert Falcon Scott thought that it would be "sublime" and "noble" to reach the South Pole by man's "own unaided efforts." He put his trust not in dogs, or his failed motorized sledges, or even his five Siberian ponies; his faith was in men's power and their unaided efforts. His decisions cost

him his life, but surely he must have known that the possibility of death was inherent to what he did, in the way he chose to lead his life.

Scott and Roald Amundsen belonged in what might be called the heroic age of exploration—when the struggle against a hostile nature was waged by individuals using mainly the weapons of physical endurance, mental fortitude, and psychological bravery—but change was in the air. Machines were on the way that would tip the balance in people's favor, tools and machines that would mitigate the bitter cold, the impassable terrain, and the isolation and long duration of the expedition. Even during the time of Douglas Mawson and Ernest Shackleton, such explorers must be put in the heroic category, too; new technology was not quite ready for their use. There were a few difficult explorations after Mawson and Shackleton, but generally speaking, none that match their explorations in hardship.

MAWSON'S ACHIEVEMENTS

When Douglas Mawson began his expedition to the southern continent in December 1911, aboard the *Aurora*, Scott was engaged in his quest for the South Pole. Mawson had been invited to participate in Scott's mission, but he had declined because he had his own scientific exploration in mind. Mawson, an Australian geologist, had accompanied Shackleton on his 1907 "farthest-south" journey, and in 1909 he had also been first at the South Magnetic Pole with Edgeworth David and Alistair Mackay. Thus, at the age of 29, Mawson was a scientist-explorer of significant Antarctic experience. Mawson's intentions in late 1911 were to explore Adélie Land (not visited since Dumont d'Urville discovered it 50 years before); he planned to send out parties to the east, the west, and south toward the Pole. This was not, however, to be an attempt at the South Pole.

Searching along the Adélie coast for a base site, he settled on Cape Denison, a rocky, uninviting spot along an icy coast largely devoid of shelter. The night of landing gave a foreshadowing of what the weather held in store for the expedition. The wind reached 70 miles per hour, and it was several days before the men could venture outside. Mawson wrote later that the average wind speed was 60 miles per hour and that the frigid blasts almost never ceased, although occasionally "an abating wind suddenly gave way to an intense, eerie silence." The Adélie coast was in fact a place where the cyclonic winds poured down from the Polar Plateau unhindered by any coastal mountains or natural obstacle. It is now known that the wind in that location is as violent as any to be found on Earth. Mawson named his base (and the book he later wrote about this expedition) the "Home of the Blizzard." The men developed strategies for coping: They learned to walk at a 45° angle into the wind and to always wear crampons and carry an ice ax; they also learned to communicate with hand gestures and signs, as there was no point in trying to hear voices in the everlasting tumult of the wind.

Somehow the men managed to build their living hut and a few buildings housing scientific equipment. They raised a radio mast time after time, only to see it ripped down by the wind. Eventually that task was securely completed, and the party settled down to wait for spring, gathered around the stove while the wind outside whipped up to 200 miles per hour.

In November 1912, five parties set out from base camp. Mawson with Lieutenant B. E. S. Ninnis and Dr. Xavier Mertz were to travel to the east, cross over two large glacier tongues (later to be named Mertz and Ninnis) and explore and chart the Oates Coast (just west of Victoria Land and the McMurdo Sound). The two glaciers were a great hazard, because Antarctic glaciers hide the trekker's worse nightmare: the crevasse. The crevasse is almost never visible; it is disguised by a thin layer of innocent-looking snow called a snow bridge. Sometimes dogs can sense a crevasse; sometimes an explorer walking in advance can tell from the sound of his or her pole striking the surface that there is a hollow beneath; sometimes there is no warning.

On December 13, Mawson readjusted the loads on the two sledges his party was using. On the rear sled he placed the tent, all the dogs' food and most of the men's food, and the most needed items. The lead sledge, the one most likely to be lost in an accident, contained a 10-day supply of food. The next day, Mertz, in the lead, identified a snow bridge, which he and Mawson crossed safely, but suddenly Ninnis and the six best dogs disappeared without

The Dry Valleys of Antarctica

A strange valley was discovered by Robert Scott in 1903 in the mountains of Victoria Land. Coming down the Ferrar Glacier, Scott and two companions entered a valley between the surrounding peaks that differed from any other area they had seen so far. There was no snow, and the temperature was relatively warm. There was no sign of animal life, although a skeleton of a seal was found. Scott was surprised to find that there was no plant life whatsoever, not even moss or lichen. There was a frozen lake in the valley, and here and there were weirdly shaped boulders, intricately carved as though by human agency.

Subsequent exploration discovered many such valleys, in all regions of Antarctica. Some valleys abounded in the rock sculptures, where abrasive sand had hollowed out and cut away portions of the stone, leaving holes and fantastical shapes; erosion of crystalline rock had caused particles to break off, leaving bizarre forms standing in beds of their own sand (eroded fragments of the rock) as if works of art in an Asian garden.

Some of the valleys were found to have rivers and lakes. In the Wright Valley, the Onyx River flows into the Vanda Lake, which has an outlet and is permanently frozen on top. The water just beneath is absolutely pure and fresh, but at the bottom of this lake is a level of saline water that has a temperature 83° Fahrenheit above the temperature of the valley around it. In this dense saline soup are algae, bacteria, and protozoa that live by recycling nutrients among them. Also in the Wright Valley is Don Juan Pond, whose surface is broken by ventifacts (stones polished by the wind). The water there is a saturated solution of calcium chloride, which serves to make the pond unfreezable, even at −60° Fahrenheit.

For some unknown reason, a number of seals and penguins wander into the dry valleys, traveling as much as 50 miles from the sea. Once in the valley, these animals die and become mummified—"freeze-dried"—and after thousands of years reduced to a skeleton.

It is hypothesized that because of the topography of the area, glacier flow was directed away from these valleys. And once the ice-snow-free area existed, the absorption of the solar heat kept the area warmer than the reflective ice areas surrounding the valley. However they were formed, the valleys are considered by scientists to be the near equivalent to a Martian landscape, and materials and vehicles have been tested in them in preparation for interplanetary exploration.

a sound: "For three hours," wrote Mawson, "we called unceasingly but no answering sound came back." There was nothing to be done but take stock of the situation, which was that they were 317 miles from base with food for 10 days and no tent. "We considered it a possibility to get through," Mawson later reflected, "but terribly handicapped," they decided to turn back: "May God help us," Mawson wrote in his diary at that time.

Mawson's journey back—alone because Mertz died soon after—is certainly one of the most terrible stories in all of polar exploration. There were times in that dreadful retreat that Mawson was tempted to give up (one was when he was hanging suspended by a rope 14 feet down the inside of a crevasse) but against all odds he returned to Cape Denison.

The 15 scientists who were on Mawson's mission produced a very substantial amount of data deemed by the international scientific community to be of great importance. Queen Mary Coast had been charted. The most difficult and hostile part of East Antarctica was now on the map. Mawson returned to Antarctica in 1929 and in 1930 on Scott's old *Discovery* and followed the coastline of King George V Land to Enderby Land, charting about 1,000 miles of the coast. All in all, Sir Douglas Mawson must be considered one of the premier explorers of Antarctica, and his contributions are equal to those of any modern human in advancing knowledge and understanding of the southern continent.

SHACKLETON'S EPIC VOYAGE

In 1911 it was still not known whether Antarctica was one massive piece of land or two large islands. There was a theory that the Weddell and Ross Seas were inlets to the continent that by means of a channel divided the continent in two. This theory could be tested by a transcontinental expedition that went from east to west passing near the South Pole. A German explorer, Wilhelm Filchner, decided to attempt this crossing in 1911, beginning from the coast of Coats Land. The *Deutsch-*

land sailed south along the coast to the Luitpold Coast, previously unknown. There, Filchner made a number of sledge journeys and discovered the vast Filchner Ice Shelf. Crossing the continent, however, was out of the question; the expedition was not outfitted for such an endeavor. After nine months of imprisonment in the ice, the *Deutschland* broke free and escaped back to Hamburg. As Filchner would write in his account of his expedition, "Admittedly, all my fine hopes and all the carefully developed plans were to be in vain."

In 1914, an attempt similar to Filchner's was being planned by Ernest Shackleton; it was being called the British Trans-Antarctic Expedition. The scope of the operation was most ambitious. Three groups, under Shackleton on board the *Endurance*, were to establish a base as far south as possible in the Weddell Sea area. From there, one party would strike out for the east, another to the west (toward Graham Land on the peninsula). The main party, led by Shackleton, was to travel due south, cross the South Pole, and approximately follow Scott's return route to McMurdo Sound. A huge portion of interior Antarctica would, as a consequence, be explored by this three-pronged attack. In vital support of Shackleton's journey, a second ship, the *Aurora,* under the command of Aeneas Mackintosh was to be sent directly to McMurdo Sound and Scott's old base; from there the crew would establish depots of food and supplies along the way to the head of the Beardmore Glacier. Shackleton would desperately need these supplies for what would be the last stage of his trek over the Pole. All kinds of scientific work were planned for all three branches of the operation.

By August 1, 1914, when Shackleton left London on the *Endurance,* the group who would sail to McMurdo Sound were already on their way to Tasmania, where they would pick up the *Aurora,* loaded and ready for their part of the vast exploration. Shackleton, with the experienced and reliable Frank Wild as his assistant, reached the South Georgia Islands (in the Scotia Sea off the southern tip of South America) at the end of October. Further south, a late winter resulted in unusually violent seas and heavy pack ice. In January 1915, Shackleton discovered a new coastline, which he named Caird Coast (after Sir James Caird, a British patron of the expedition). As the *Endurance* struggled further south in the Weddell Sea, the ice became more and more impossible. Finally, approaching the coast of Luitpold Land, 80 miles off shore, the *Endurance* became fast in the ice, never to be free again.

Very rapidly, the situation of the doomed ship became precarious, listing one way and then heaved over the other as huge pressure ridges twisted and crushed the helpless wooden ship from all sides. The movement of the ice in this area was relentless; as Shackleton would write in his classic account of this expedition, *South,* "We seem to be drifting helplessly in a strange world of unreality." The *Endurance* had come to a halt on January 19, 1915; by October 26, 1915, the ship had been trapped by the ice floes for some 280 days, during which time the ship, ice, and men had moved 573 miles to the northwest. That very day the men began to evacuate the ship; supplies were unloaded, and the men were soon living on the ice in what Shackleton, in *South,* called Ocean Camp. Among the items saved were 120 glass plates with photographs taken by Frank Hurley; these would provide dramatic documentation of the expedition.

Shackleton knew they should strike out for land somewhere, but with 28 men and three ship's boats weighting more than a ton each, movement and travel was next to impossible.

Ernest Shackleton recounted his epic voyage on the *Endurance* between 1914 and 1916 in *South,* an exploration classic. *(Library of Congress, Prints and Photographs Division [LC-USZ62-85042])*

Attempts to move overland by pulling the boats and supplies by dogs and men never resulted in more than one mile per day due to the condition of the ice. On November 21, as Shackleton later described himself calling out "She's gone, boys," the *Endurance* sank, and the men were alone on the frozen Antarctic Ocean. On New Year's Day 1916, the crew celebrated by having cups of cocoa all around. It was the last of that delicacy. The men were not yet starving; now and then a seal or penguin was shot. But one by one, the dogs were killed and eaten. "It was the worst job," wrote Shackleton in *South,* "that we had throughout the Expedition." The next four months were a nightmare of living on breaking up ice floes and narrow escapes in the three boats when they entered water leads as they opened up.

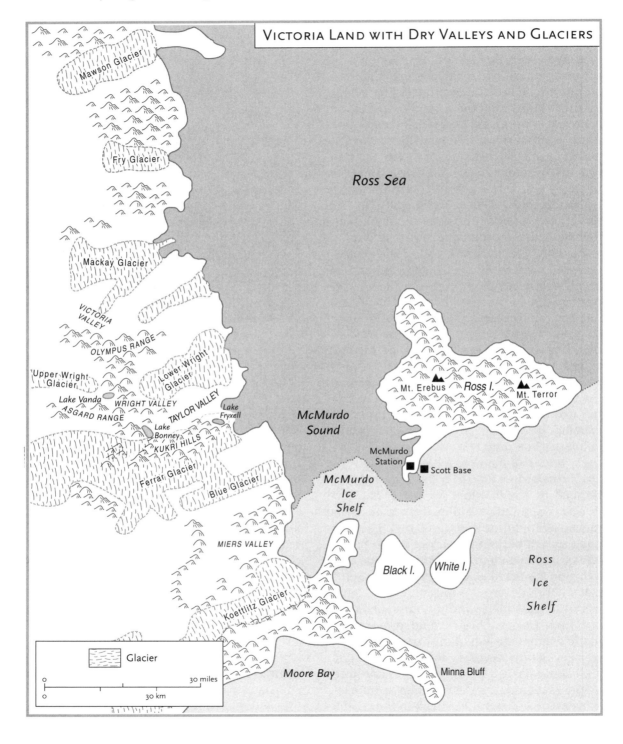

VICTORIA LAND WITH DRY VALLEYS AND GLACIERS

Mawson Glacier

Fry Glacier

Ross Sea

Mackay Glacier

VICTORIA
VALLEY

OLYMPUS RANGE

Upper Wright
Glacier

Lower Wright
Glacier

Lake Vanda

WRIGHT VALLEY

Lake
Fryxell

ASGARD RANGE

TAYLOR VALLEY

Lake
Bonney

KUKRI HILLS

Ferrar Glacier

Blue Glacier

MIERS VALLEY

Koettlitz Glacier

Moore Bay

McMurdo
Sound

Mt. Erebus   Ross I.   Mt. Terror

McMurdo
Station

Scott Base

McMurdo
Ice
Shelf

Ross
Ice
Shelf

Black I.

White I.

Minna Bluff

Glacier

30 miles

30 km

The goal had become to reach Elephant Island, a barren rocky place off the tip of the Antarctic Peninsula.

On April 15, 1916, the island was sighted and with great difficulty, the three boats were landed, despite the reefs, rocky shoals, and pounding surf. The men poured out of the boats, and many kissed the barren inhospitable beach; after all, it had been a year and a half since they had set foot on land. That night, wrote Shackleton, the men enjoyed a "safe and glorious sleep." On April 24, Shackleton set out with five handpicked men in one of the small boats, promising to return with a rescue ship.

It is interesting to consider the character of the man who had thus far been able to avoid what could have been a disaster of great proportions. Shackleton had first come to Antarctica as an adventurer, a man who by his own admission wanted to make a "bit of money." To better understand Shackleton's actions after landing on Elephant Island, one must take note of the transformation in character that had occurred over the years. There had been leaders over the centuries, in the Arctic and in the Antarctic, who were men of intelligence and imagination, men who inspired their crews to bravery and endurance through their own behavior. And there had been leaders who, because of their incompetence, their arrogance, and their selfishness, had brought about the ruin of both their missions and the confidence and competence of their followers. Shackleton was a man who became famous and beloved not only by his men but by all the seafaring community as well. He was a leader—"the Boss"—and took upon himself the absolute responsibility for the well-being of his crew. This attitude, this sense of duty, was, without being specifically articulated, understood by the crew of the *Endurance* and even of the *Aurora*. So his men knew he would

get them off the ice, to Elephant Island, and they knew when he left them there to go for help that he would return. "Lash up and stow, boys, the Boss may come today," was Frank Wild's wake-up call every morning to the men stranded on Elephant Island.

And one day, August 30, 1916, a ship appeared and a small boat pulled toward shore. A man was standing on the bow; it was the Boss. His first words showed what had been his foremost thought during the 128 days of his absence: "Are you all well?" And the answer was, "We are all well, Boss."

Shackleton had made the voyage from Elephant Island to the whaling station at South Georgia Islands through 800 miles of the most storm-ridden seas in the world, in a 22-foot open boat. There followed a grueling two-day hike overland to a Norwegian whaling station. It then took four attempts to get through the ice back to Elephant Island.

While the ambitious aims of the trans-Antarctic mission had not been met, Shackleton's 1914 expedition has been called a "glorious failure." Shackleton did not return immediately to war-torn Europe; he hastened to McMurdo Sound in aid of that section of his exploratory party. They had had a dreadful time, and two members of the expedition did not survive. When he did finally return to England, Shackleton served in World War I. After the war, Sir Ernest Shackleton set off on another polar mission in 1921, but at Grytviken, South Georgia, near where he had landed from Elephant Island, he quite suddenly died, at age 48. He is buried there, beneath the mountains he crossed to seek rescue for his comrades.

AERIAL EXPLORATION

It would be more than 40 years later that a land expedition accomplished a trans-Antarctic

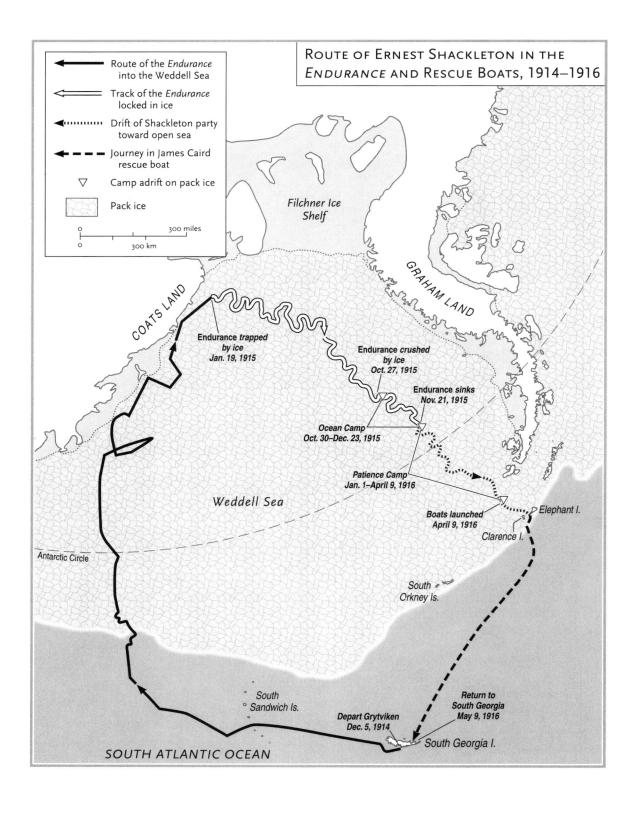

Route of Ernest Shackleton in the *Endurance* and Rescue Boats, 1914–1916

Legend

→ Route of the *Endurance* into the Weddell Sea
⇐ Track of the *Endurance* locked in ice
◀·········· Drift of Shackleton party toward open sea
◀ ─ ─ Journey in James Caird rescue boat
▽ Camp adrift on pack ice
▭ Pack ice

300 miles
300 km

Filchner Ice Shelf

GRAHAM LAND

COATS LAND

Endurance *trapped by ice* Jan. 19, 1915

Endurance *crushed by ice* Oct. 27, 1915

Endurance *sinks* Nov. 21, 1915

Ocean Camp Oct. 30–Dec. 23, 1915

Patience Camp Jan. 1–April 9, 1916

Weddell Sea

Boats launched April 9, 1916

Elephant I.

Clarence I.

Antarctic Circle

South Orkney Is.

South Sandwich Is.

Return to South Georgia May 9, 1916

Depart Grytviken Dec. 5, 1914

South Georgia I.

SOUTH ATLANTIC OCEAN

crossing as attempted by Filchner and Shackleton. In the meantime, the airplane was gradually becoming the primary tool for exploration. A low-flying plane could photograph and map an area of undiscovered territory in 20 minutes that a land party might spend three months doing. Experiments in mechanized land vehicles—snow tractors, cars, and even mobile laboratories—had all largely been failures. But the airplane, from its earliest use, proved to be reliable and adaptable to all phases of exploration. The idea of using the airplane to assist surface travel by laying out routes and dropping depots began to seem to explorers to be a perfect blend of the old ways and the new technology. One of the very first people to use the airplane to discover new territories was Australian Hubert Wilkins.

Wilkins had been a member of Shackleton's final polar mission in 1921, and he had experience flying in the Canadian Arctic; he had also spent a number of years as a professional photographer. He was thus an able pioneer in Antarctic air exploration, even though he was a bit of an adventurer and by no means a scientist. In 1928, he set up a base on the north coast of the peninsula, and in that year and the next, he flew over and photographed (and drew pictures of) almost 1,500 miles of the Antarctic Peninsula. Wilkins's work provided later aviators with two important facts: Flying in Antarctica was completely dependent on good weather; second, the bigger and heavier the airplane, the better.

COMMANDER RICHARD BYRD

The next aerial exploration was much more massive and ambitious than that of Wilkins, and it was undertaken by a man whose drive, bravery, and leadership matched that of any

Richard Evelyn Byrd's flights over the North and South Poles signaled a new era of Arctic exploration that would treat airplanes as as integral element. *(Library of Congress, Prints and Photographs Division [LC-USZ62-108373])*

Antarctic explorer of his time. A U.S. Navy officer, Richard Evelyn Byrd had already shown his mettle by flying over the North Pole in 1926. Byrd plotted his 1928 expedition with great care. He planned to fly to the South Pole, but he also intended to do a major aerial reconnaissance of the continent. On the advice of Amundsen, he took along 95 dogs. Later, in his account of this expedition, *Little America,* he wrote: "I can see now that the wisest thing we ever did was to insist on bringing them." His two ships, *City of New York* and

Eleanor Bolling, had a strange hybrid cargo of the old and the new: dogs, three airplanes, and tons of coal and airplane fuel. Other incongruous items were 1,200 boots and 1,200 pounds of cookies.

Byrd left New Zealand in summer 1928 and just after Christmas settled on a spot for his base near the Bay of Whales, to the east of the Ross Ice Shelf. By January 1, 1929, a station was built, Little America, with three main buildings, many small huts for research use, three hangars, storage places for airplane fuel, and a cluster of high radio masts. In mid-January, Byrd made his first flight, a test run of about an hour. In that brief time he was able to photograph 1,000 square miles of Antarctic territory never seen before.

During winter 1929, the expedition prepared both for the polar flight and for the several land excursions that would explore the Queen Maud Mountains, as well as the rough flight path of the airplane. Byrd planned every aspect of the intended flight with the meticulous precision that had become his trademark. The winter passed uneventfully, with the men comfortably dug into their cavelike quarters, enjoying an abundance of food and in easy radio contact with New York. On September 1, they learned that the temperature in New York City was 94° Fahrenheit;

WINTER HEADQUARTERS BASE
EDGAR G. BARRATT, CONSULTING ENGINEER—WILLIAMS and BARRATT, ARCHITECTS

1 EXECUTIVE OFFICE, LABORATORY, RADIO, DOCTOR
2 MESS ROOM and KITCHEN
3 and 4 BUNK HOUSES
5 MACHINE SHOP - ELECTRIC GENERATOR
6 WEATHER STATION
7 COVERED PLANES
8 MAGNETISM OBSERVATORY

BYRD ANTARCTIC EXPEDITION

After being the first to fly over the North Pole in 1926, Richard Evelyn Byrd navigated the first flight over the South Pole in 1929. This latter expedition's winter headquarters are depicted in this drawing.
(Library of Congress, Prints and Photographs Division [LC-USZ62-119044])

Visiting his hometown of Boston after his successful South Pole flight, Richard Evelyn Byrd was honored with a parade. *(Library of Congress, Prints and Photographs Division [LC-USZ62-113390])*

outside the radio hut the thermometer read –63° Fahrenheit.

In spring, the land parties began leaving in October on motor sledges that lasted 80 miles before they broke down. Then the dogs took over. On November 28, the weather was fine at Little America, and the Queen Maud land party radioed in that the weather was fine and clear at and beyond the mountains ringing the central plateau (on which the Pole was situated). The Ford trimotor monoplane took off for the Pole after noon, with Byrd as navigator,

Bernt Balchen as pilot, Harold June as radio operator, and Ashley McKinley as photographer. There were some terrifying moments: In order to get through the mountains, the flyers had to jettison everything that might have helped them survive, had they been forced to come down. But they reached the plateau safely and at 1:14 A.M. they passed over the Pole. The explorers returned to Little America on November 29, 1929. Byrd had been the first to fly over the North Pole and had now duplicated the feat at the South Pole. What

Amundsen and Scott had done in months, Byrd had accomplished in 16 hours, during which time he had seen (and photographed) more than Scott and Amundsen had encountered in their entire careers. The *New York Times* observed, "a new dimension has been added to the exploration of our planet." Byrd did not think that his historic flight was his greatest achievement; rather, he believed that opening up new dimensions in exploration by means of the airplane was his contribution to human progress. And certainly, he had done this; from this point on, there would be no significant exploration in Antarctica that did not involve the use of the airplane.

EXPLORATION CONTINUES

An interesting and important, although minor, expedition was undertaken in 1934–37 by Australian John Rymill. In 1926, Wilkins, while flying over the Antarctic Peninsula, had reported seeing three straits running across Graham Land that appeared to divide the peninsula into segments. Thus it might be that the peninsula was in fact a number of large islands. With a ground-based operation (and dogs) and a small single-engine airplane, Rymill did a thorough exploration of Graham Land, the part of the peninsula that was very little known, and proved that there were no channels from the east to the west coast of Graham Land. Rymill's three-year expedition was remarkable because it was carried out by men who were all "amateurs" at polar exploration.

As Rymill was exploring in Graham Land, an American flyer and explorer was preparing to make the first transcontinental flight of Antarctica. Lincoln Ellsworth, who had flown over the North Pole with Amundsen and Umberto Nobile in 1926, was a millionaire adventurer whose first love was the legendary

cowboy Marshall Wyatt Earp. He was also an intrepid flyer, and after a number of false starts and bad weather breaks, in November 1935, Ellsworth succeeded in flying from the northern tip of the Antarctic Peninsula to the Ross Ice Barrier, just 16 miles from the deserted Little America base. Here, Ellsworth landed his plane for the last time on December 5. The petrol, 466 gallons, was gone, and the airplane was useless. Ellsworth managed to make his way to one of the Little America buildings. After a month, he was rescued by the RRS *Discovery II* and his own ship, the *Wyatt Earp*. Still in his possession were Earp's gun holster and wedding ring, his good luck charms. He had flown 2,300 miles and become the first to cross the Antarctic Continent by air.

In 1934, meanwhile, Byrd had constructed an advance weather station 125 miles south of his base, Little America II; at the last minute, he decided to spend the winter there alone. As recounted in his book *Alone*, he nearly died there because of a breakdown in the ventilation system. After he was rescued, the expedition continued to carry out its objectives. More than 450,000 square miles of land were surveyed, and a wealth of geological and meteorological data was accumulated. Five years later, Byrd returned to Antarctica on the *North Star*, on a mission solidly supported by the U.S. government. This expedition also brought back an abundance of geographical information, ensuring that Byrd would be considered the greatest contributor ever to the Antarctic map.

ANTARCTICA BECOMES INTERNATIONAL

In the background of Byrd's third expedition (1939–41), there were troublesome rumblings of international dissent about sovereignty in regard to the southern continent. Argentina

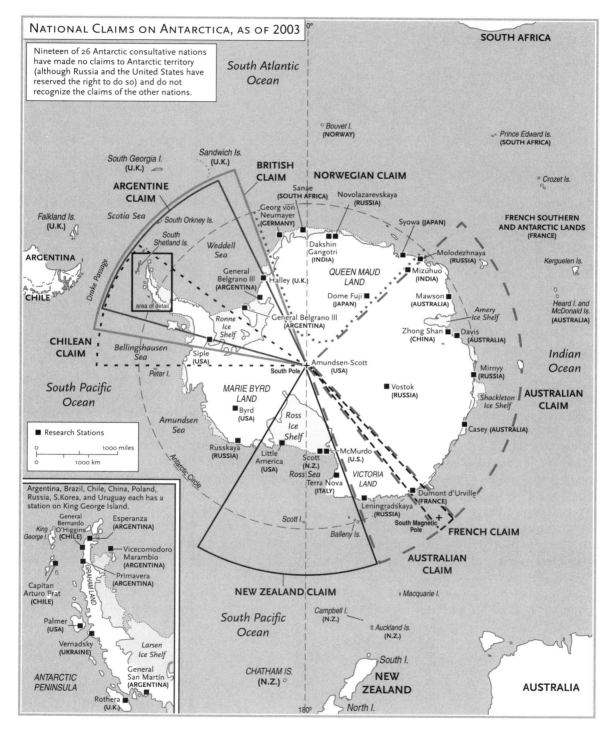

NATIONAL CLAIMS ON ANTARCTICA, AS OF 2003

Nineteen of 26 Antarctic consultative nations have made no claims to Antarctic territory (although Russia and the United States have reserved the right to do so) and do not recognize the claims of the other nations.

0°

SOUTH AFRICA

South Atlantic Ocean

Bouvet I. (NORWAY)

Prince Edward Is. (SOUTH AFRICA)

Crozet Is.

Sandwich Is. (U.K.)

South Georgia I. (U.K.)

BRITISH CLAIM

NORWEGIAN CLAIM

ARGENTINE CLAIM

Sanae (SOUTH AFRICA)

Novolazarevskaya (RUSSIA)

Syowa (JAPAN)

FRENCH SOUTHERN AND ANTARCTIC LANDS (FRANCE)

Falkland Is. (U.K.)

Scotia Sea

South Orkney Is.

Georg von Neumayer (GERMANY)

Molodezhnaya (RUSSIA)

Kerguelen Is.

ARGENTINA

South Shetland Is.

Weddell Sea

Dakshin Gangotri (INDIA)

QUEEN MAUD LAND

Mizuho (INDIA)

Drake Passage

area of detail

General Belgrano III (ARGENTINA)

Halley (U.K.)

Dome Fuji (JAPAN)

Mawson (AUSTRALIA)

Amery Ice Shelf

Heard I. and McDonald Is. (AUSTRALIA)

CHILE

CHILEAN CLAIM

Ronne Ice Shelf

General Belgrano III (ARGENTINA)

Zhong Shan (CHINA)

Davis (AUSTRALIA)

Indian Ocean

Bellingshausen Sea

Siple (USA)

Amundsen-Scott (USA)

South Pole

AUSTRALIAN CLAIM

Peter I.

South Pacific Ocean

MARIE BYRD LAND

Vostok (RUSSIA)

Mirnyy (RUSSIA)

Shackleton Ice Shelf

Amundsen Sea

Byrd (USA)

Ross Ice Shelf

Casey (AUSTRALIA)

■ Research Stations

1000 miles
1000 km

Russkaya (RUSSIA)

Little America (USA)

Scott (N.Z.)

McMurdo (U.S.)

Terra Nova (ITALY)

VICTORIA LAND

Dumont d'Urville (FRANCE)

Antarctic Circle

Ross Sea

Leningradskaya (RUSSIA)

South Magnetic Pole

FRENCH CLAIM

Argentina, Brazil, Chile, China, Poland, Russia, S.Korea, and Uruguay each has a station on King George Island.

Scott I.

Balleny Is.

AUSTRALIAN CLAIM

General Bernardo O'Higgins (CHILE)

Esperanza (ARGENTINA)

NEW ZEALAND CLAIM

Macquarie I.

King George I.

South Pacific Ocean

Campbell I. (N.Z.)

Vicecomodoro Marambio (ARGENTINA)

Auckland Is. (N.Z.)

GRAHAM LAND

Primavera (ARGENTINA)

Capitán Arturo Prat (CHILE)

South I.

Palmer (USA)

Larsen Ice Shelf

NEW ZEALAND

AUSTRALIA

Vernadsky (UKRAINE)

General San Martín (ARGENTINA)

ANTARCTIC PENINSULA

CHATHAM IS. (N.Z.)

North I.

Rothera (U.K.)

180°

made proclamations and expeditions; Chile, Great Britain, and Germany joined in making aggressive actions and edicts and claiming slices of the Antarctic Continent. To this end, the U.S. Navy in 1946 appointed Admiral Richard Byrd head of Operation Highjump, which sailed to Antarctica with 13 ships, 23 planes, several helicopters, and 4,700 men, of whom only 24 were civilian scientists (the rest were military personnel).

Permanent stations manned by various countries proliferated during the 1940s and 1950s. Argentina, Chile, France, the United States, Britain, Norway, Sweden, and the Soviet Union, among others, rushed to establish bases that were scientific in purpose while also staking claim to territory. Some kind of international oversight and governance was clearly needed.

A first step toward international communication was taken when the International Council of Scientific Unions suggested that the International Polar Year, scheduled for 1983, be moved forward and renamed the International Geophysical Year (IGY). The two topics in focus for the 18-month study were designated as outer space and Antarctica. The plan was enthusiastically accepted by interested countries; there was a flurry of activity in preparation for 1957, and by the time the conference began, there were 40 (mostly permanent) stations on the continent and 20 more on the subantarctic islands, all staffed by scientists busily preparing their reports and presentations.

A significant piece of exploration was the indirect result of the heightened activity preceding the IGY. Briton Vivian Fuchs and New Zealander Sir Edmund Hillary (knighted for his ascent of Mount Everest in 1953) teamed up to achieve the first transcontinental surface crossing, from the Weddell Sea to the Ross Sea via the South Pole. The Fuchs party consisted of 10 men and eight motorized vehicles designed to travel over snow and ice: four Sno-Cats (heavy-duty treaded vehicles), three Weasels (lighter treaded vehicles), and a muskeg tractor (a farm tractor, modified to move through deep snow or over ice). Hillary established depots from McMurdo Sound to the Pole; the two explorers met at the Pole and Fuchs continued on to the base at Pram Point on McMurdo Sound, reaching there in February 1958 after a trek of 99 days and 2,158 miles.

Coming out of the very successful IGY, and at the instigation of U.S. president Dwight D. Eisenhower, was a determination to create a permanent accord between nations in regard to Antarctica. Consequently, in October 1959, 12 nations met and hammered out one of the most incredible documents in human history asserting international accord, cooperation, and unity: the Antarctica Treaty. The opening sentence of the preamble presents the significant message of the treaty: "[I]t is in the interest of all mankind that Antarctica shall continue forever to be used exclusively for peaceful purposes and shall not become the scene or object of international discord." Thus was it assured, in a moment of international wisdom and political disinterestedness, that Antarctica would be the haven for scientific work that would help provide all the people of the world with knowledge of their world—past, present, and future.

10

THE EVOLUTION
OF POLAR EXPLORATION

The great Arctic explorer Vilhjalmur Stefansson did not believe that reaching the North Pole should be the exclusive goal of Arctic exploration. Rather, he believed that the responsibility of the serious polar explorer was to lay the groundwork for future discoveries, in whatever way possible. This attitude should serve as a reminder that the attainment of the North Pole as well as that of the South Pole was the culmination of centuries of Arctic and Antarctic activity and exploration. Getting to the North and South Poles was an expression of personal ambition for those intrepid adventurers who attempted it. Genuine exploration has behind it a more impersonal quest for knowledge and understanding of things not yet found or understood.

At the same time, it should not be assumed that the spirit of exploration is necessarily a pure, lofty, noble thing. As this account has shown, there has usually been some more mundane reason why explorers went off into the unknown. Perhaps it was a story about a sea passage that led from England directly to the riches of the Far East, or an abundance of rich furs, whales, or seals that enticed seamen and traders to go where there were no maps—where no one had gone before. The profit motive was certainly behind the expeditions that went in search of the Northwest Passage; the profit motive was a strong factor in the voyages of the whalers and sealers who sailed the Antarctic seas and first set foot on Antarctica.

What is significant about polar exploration, however, is that inevitably the profit motive was left behind or at least became secondary to something that was more quintessential. A captain who sailed into an unknown sea might have been hungry for the profits of whaling, but he was also an explorer. Ernest Shackleton, for example, first went to Antarctica as an adventurer, to make a little money. He ended up as one of the greatest heroic explorers of all time. So, it is necessary to live with the paradox of the mixed motives of many explorers who went into the polar

139

Seals were merely one of the animals in the polar regions hunted for profit. *(Library of Congress, Prints and Photographs Division [LOT 11453-1, no. 418])*

regions. Hand in hand with the desire to make money was another motive—the lure of the frontier.

THE MOTIVE FORCES

There have always been those human beings, bold and restless in nature, who were dissatisfied within the bounds of the safe, known world. Perhaps it is basic human nature to strive to know the nature of the physical Earth, as though this knowledge will somehow bring understanding to the whole evolution and destiny of humankind. Long before the Northwest Passage was finally found, it was known that it was too frozen to be useful, yet the search continued with increased fervor. Why did the quest for the North Pole attract generations of explorers, leading many of them to their deaths? The Inuit knew that there was

nothing there and, in their practical interpretation of human activity, thought the explorers' mania for that desolate, useless spot was madness. The lure of the frontier does not have to have a tangible objective. It is simply the desire to go beyond the edge of what is known. And there is a particular satisfaction in being the first to do so.

In all Arctic and Antarctic exploration, being the first to see ("discover") something or to perform some feat was the most important, driving goal. It is hardly noted who was the *second* person to reach the North Pole, or the *second* visitor to fly across the Antarctic Continent. Accounts of polar exploration are full of "farthest norths" and "farthest souths" and "firsts to reach" and "firsts to cross." James Burney, an officer under Captain James Cook on the *Adventure*, in his published journal recounted Cook's words when encountering the ice off Antarctica in 1772: "I, who had ambition not only to go farther than any one had been before, but as far as it was possible for man to go, was not sorry at meeting this interruption." The attitude reflected here is a typical one for the polar explorer: He or she may not have reached his or her goal but had still gone farther than anyone else had done. He or she had a "first." Many American polar explorers, such as Isaac Hayes, did not even intend to try for the North Pole; they were sat-

Louise Boyd searched for Roald Amundsen after he was lost in the Arctic in 1928 and completed a 16-hour flight over the North Pole in 1955. Like many before her, she found the lure of the Arctic irresistible. *(Library of Congress, Prints and Photographs Division [LC-USZ62-119368])*

isfied with a "farthest north" because that ensured them a hero's welcome upon their return.

Many of the explorers who were the first to visit uncharted, even unknown places, speak of the thrill of discovery. What fabulous things there were to see, things never seen before by European eyes! Sir Martin Frobisher in 1576 sailing into a bay of Baffin Island and convinced that he was seeing America to the west and Asia to the east; members of James Clark Ross's expedition in 1841 experiencing the grandeur of the Transantarctic Mountains— these are but two of many moments in polar exploration that, for the explorers involved, justified all the preceding hardships. In a multitude of small ways the thrill of discovery was felt by all polar explorers: herds of reindeer on the Siberian tundra, the aurora borealis, the Inuit snow house, the antics of penguins, a polar bear with a cub, and the calving of an iceberg. All these things and a thousand others were new and amazing to the explorers' eyes.

It was not only the spectacle of new sights that rewarded the polar traveler; the Arctic and the Antarctic, for those who were open to it, were regions of strange and eerie beauty. The thousands of drawings and paintings, and later photographs, are evidence of how impressed the generations of explorers were with the pristine beauty of the polar regions. It was as though the explorer was seeing nature in its purest forms: powerful and indifferent to the puny attempts of people to master it.

It is notable that many expeditions of the 19th and 20th centuries took along artists, and later photographers, whose job was not just to record the achievements of the mission but also to immortalize the sights that so impressed the explorers. Interestingly, many of the drawings were of storms at sea, towering black mountains of ocean about to descend on

Polar bears are one of the animals encountered by explorers that must have intrigued them and fueled their urge to continue. *(Cyberphoto)*

the frail, wind-tossed vessels. Other favorite scenes were depictions of the pack ice jammed up into pressure ridges higher than the ship, threatening to smash the imprisoned intruding ship into matchsticks. Many an artist also painted the setting arctic sun, a sunset that presaged six months of darkness to come before sunrise. The sun is a thing of rare beauty when it will not be seen again for half a year; a storm at sea is an awesome and terrible thing of beauty when it is survived, and seamen can later boast of getting the best of nature at its worst. There were softer, more ordinary beautiful things in the polar regions, too. The Arctic has more than 1,000 varieties of flowers that in the brief summer bring a carpet of color to many of the Arctic islands. The ever-changing colors of a crystal-like Antarctic iceberg is a memorable sight. And many explorers have written about the beauty of the arctic winter night, when beneath the sky emblazoned with countless bright stars, the air is so clear and cold that the observer seems to be seeing and hearing forever.

But all beauty in the polar regions is tinged with danger and death. The towering black wave, the flowers that will soon die, and the clear arctic night (which indicates a drop in temperature) represent the paradoxical power of the regions to attract and repel. There were only a few polar explorers who did not fear the dangers of their expeditions. But there were fewer, or perhaps none, who came back from a polar expedition and announced, "I never want to go there again."

Understanding the lure that the Arctic and the Antarctic had for explorers is difficult, particularly when it appears that the rewards of discovery and the thrill of finding new, beautiful things were always intermixed with the possibility of disaster and death. There is no doubt that polar exploration was popular with the explorers themselves and with the populace that eagerly awaited the news of discoveries and could be counted on to welcome the return of their heroes with parades, honors, and fame. There were times when in England, continental Europe, and the United States a preoccupation with domestic affairs brought about a temporary pause in exploration activity. But time and again, a new approach, a new route, or a new nautical development rekindled the flame of expedition.

FOREKNOWLEDGE AND PREPARATION

The expeditions of the 17th century could be excused for not realizing how cold the Arctic was and how likely their ships were to be frozen in over the winter, but how does one explain why Sir John Franklin's party, in 1845, wore top hats on the ice? And how could a newspaper man from Cincinnati like Charles F. Hall, who had never been further north than Vermont, undertake an expedition to the North Pole? It is hard to imagine any

Unpreparedness

The plain fact is that the early explorers were hardly prepared for Arctic exploration. To begin with, they were without charts and maps and had no real sense of the weather conditions they would encounter. How long was an arctic summer? Explorers were to find that they were very short, as they spent an unexpected winter frozen in ice eight feet thick and that daily threatened to crush their fragile wooden sailing vessels. Changes in the severity of arctic winters were likewise an unknown factor that doomed many expeditions: A passage might be open for one winter and then impassable for the next five.

In addition, there was no effective communication. If a ship were frozen in or lost, it might easily be a year before that was known and another year before a search was begun. Often the search vessel would be marooned or lost as well. Navigational instruments and skills were not adequate for Arctic travel, and the ships themselves were not made to withstand the destructive force of arctic storms and ice packs that could crush like eggshells the frail wooden planks of the deck and hull.

In the early decades of Artic exploration, very little was known about the clothing required for Arctic travel. Wool was the preferred material ("good English worsted"), but once wool becomes wet and freezes, it is useless. It would not be until the mid-18th century that explorers copied the Inuit and changed to

(continues)

Explorers of the North Polar Region learned much from the Inuit. However, they did not adopt the Inuit's essential fur clothing until the mid-18th century. These Inuit were photographed in the early 20th century. *(Library of Congress, Prints and Photographs Division [LOT 11453-3, no. 32])*

(continued)

animal skins and furs. Even then, food was a problem. Scurvy killed more Arctic mariners than did cold and exposure. Franklin, in 1845, carried a three-year supply of rations, including 1,000 pounds of raisins, 900 pounds of lemon juice, and 170 gallons of cranberries. These items were to prevent scurvy. But in the 17th century, such stocks of fruit were not taken, and the result was an outbreak of the disease on almost every mission of any duration.

Thus it was that many of the expeditions, which set out for the exploration of the north and the search for the passage, were doomed to failure from the beginning. Some of the expeditions, unfit for their tasks, limped back to Europe with no success. Others ended tragically, with great loss of life. Success went to those explorations where the ingenuity and perseverance of the leader was a match for the unexpected and unfamiliar hazards of the Arctic territory.

geographical regions more difficult for exploration than the polar regions.

In modern times, with airplanes; radio, radar, and GPS (global positioning system); and snowmobiles, it is different. But before the 20th century, just getting to the Arctic and Antarctica was an ordeal that brought about the failure of many expeditions. There is no other form of exploration where mistakes are so likely to result in casualties. There were those explorers who understood and accepted the inherent danger of polar exploration. Robert Peary, when his crippled feet were referred to, always replied: "What are eight toes, compared to the Pole?" And Franklin, at 60 years old, had already suffered through a disastrous mission in the Canadian Arctic when he demanded to be made leader of his famous final exploration, from which he never returned. It is safe to say that explorers of the 18th century and later were knowledgeable about the hardships they would face, and the knowledge did not deter them.

Certainly there were no illusions about the conditions to be found at the South Pole.

Anyone who got through the pack ice surrounding the southern continent had already experienced the worst weather the planet had to offer; there was no reason to suppose that the continent itself would be any better. It turned out, in fact to be more terrible than could be imagined. The Russian station Vostok, located on the central plateau, has recorded temperatures of –130° Fahrenheit and lower (–100° Fahrenheit is considered a balmy day there). But explorers learned to live under these and other hostile conditions, adapting just as the expeditions to the Arctic eventually had, with better ships, better protective clothing, and eating raw seal meat to ward off scurvy.

Despite the hardships and the constant possibility of disaster, the explorers of the polar regions persevered. Great credit must be given to the courageous leaders and generations of hearty crewmen who time and time again ventured into regions where certain hardship and possible death could be the outcome. But hardship and obstacles could be overcome and disaster and death averted; with a little luck, success and discovery might reward the dedicated labors of the heroic explorer.

THE PRESENT AND THE FUTURE OF THE ARCTIC

The use and the administration of the Arctic was subjected to major disruptive forces in the 20th century, forces that might have turned the region into an international battlefield of claims, counterclaims, and divisive disharmony. Yet two cataclysmic world wars and the cold war between the United States and the Soviet Union were survived. Attempts to make the Arctic a repository for weapons of warfare and defense systems had to be dealt with. (Since 1951, the United States has maintained an air force base and ballistic missile early warning radar at Thule, Greenland.) Disputes over fishing rights, conservation, and oil and mineral exploration and exploitation had to be settled. But as the Arctic nations began to realize how the climatic, biological, geological, and other scientific studies of the Arctic were important to the world at large, a cooperative spirit began to emerge.

In 1990, the International Arctic Science Committee (IASC) was formed and had the same unifying effect that the International Polar Year (1882–83) had had. All forms of Arctic research were encouraged and facilitated thereby; all the major nations of the world, not just those in the polar region,

Countries have established many bases and research stations in Antarctica such as the Amundsen-Scott Base established by the U.S. Operation Deepfreeze. The two ships in the background participated in this operation. *(Library of Congress, Prints and Photographs Division [LC-USZ62-98698])*

participated in this organization. In 1991, the Arctic Environmental Protection Strategy (AEPS) was established and is effectively dedicated to the preservation of all aspects of the environment in the Arctic. Among other steps the AEPS has taken is to designate areas of unique ecological systems or of some other interest to scientific investigation and grant them special protection. These two agencies, it is to be noted, are nongovernmental; thus they are by design nonpolitical and have international cooperation, not competition, as their preferred approach.

The placing of research stations in the Arctic is somewhat of a problem because the Arctic is largely water, not land. The Soviets had a floating "drift station" from 1937 to 1991; most of the stations are located on the rim of the Arctic Ocean, but all are at or above the Arctic Circle. The Canadians have stations at Resolute Bay (Cornwallis Island) and on the shore of the Beaufort Sea. Of primary interest to the latter is a study of the continental shelf. The Americans have, among others, stations at Toolik Lake (Alaska) and Barrow (Alaska) on the Beaufort Sea. These research centers are involved in a huge range of studies, from Arctic ecosystems to marine and terrestrial biology and climatology. Russia, Sweden, Norway, Finland, Denmark, and Iceland also maintain stations throughout the Arctic, each with its own range of special interests in the multitude of scientific fields available.

Along with the hard scientific data that now pours out of the Arctic comes information about the history, evolution, and characteristics of the Arctic peoples. Studies in anthropology, archaeology, economics, geography, history, linguistics, and sociology are carried on by scholars in major universities, not just those within the Arctic countries.

Various experts have done extensive work on the literature written in and about the Arctic. A great deal has been written about the history of Inuit art, and an industry has developed in the collection and distribution of ancient and contemporary objects of art, from jewelry and handicrafts to soapstone carvings and other kinds of Inuit artworks. All in all, an enormous wealth of knowledge has resulted from the opening of the Arctic; such knowledge, as it should be, is the aftermath of exploration.

THE PRESENT AND THE FUTURE OF ANTARCTICA

The establishment of bases and research stations on Antarctica was a different procedure from such activity in the Arctic. From the beginning of polar exploration, wintering on the southern continent was a necessary tactic because of its location and the difficulty of getting to it through the surrounding ice pack. Explorers as early as Jules-Sébastien-César Dumont d'Urville thought to establish a base for current and future operations, and Robert Falcon Scott's base was in use for many years and many explorations. Such bases were supplied by ships, and later airplanes, that returned to more temperate headquarters (such as New Zealand). The intrepid explorers left behind learned how to survive the cold winters, most often burrowing into quarters under snow or ice. The International Geophysical Year of 1957–58 had brought about the American Operation Deepfreeze, which had resulted in the building of the Amundsen-Scott Base at the South Pole. At about the same time, the Soviets had established Sovietskaya base and, later, Vostok (on the Polar Plateau, the coldest place on Earth). By 1971 there were more than 40 occupied stations on Antarctica, well attended by aircraft and all

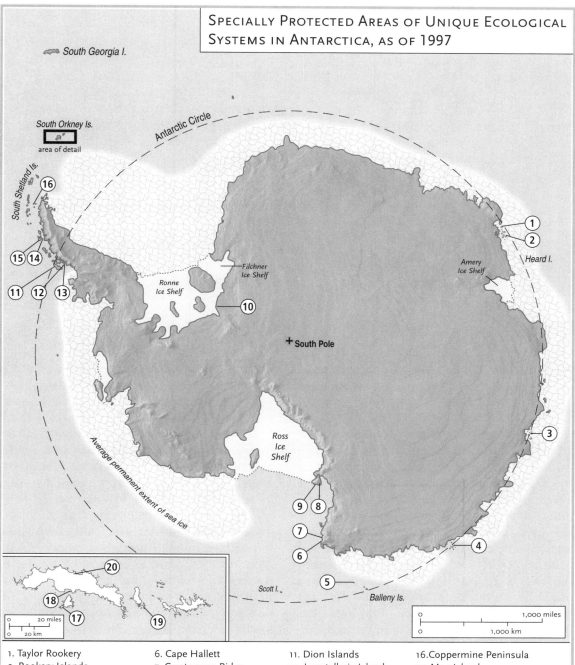

SPECIALLY PROTECTED AREAS OF UNIQUE ECOLOGICAL SYSTEMS IN ANTARCTICA, AS OF 1997

South Georgia I.

South Orkney Is.

area of detail

South Shetland Is.

Antarctic Circle

Filchner
Ice Shelf

Ronne
Ice Shelf

Amery
Ice Shelf

Heard I.

+ South Pole

Ross
Ice
Shelf

Average permanent extent of sea ice

Scott I.

Balleny Is.

20 miles
20 km

0   1,000 miles
0   1,000 km

1. Taylor Rookery
2. Rookery Islands
3. Ardery Island, Odbert Island
4. Pointe Géologie Archipelago
5. Sabrina Island

6. Cape Hallett
7. Cryptogram Ridge
8. New College Valley
9. Beaufort Island
10. Forlidas Pond,
     Davis Valley Ponds

11. Dion Islands
12. Lagotellerie Island
13. Avian Island
14. Green Island
15. Litchfield Island

16. Coppermine Peninsula
17. Moe Island
18. Lynch Island
19. Southern Powell Island,
     adjacent islands
20. Northern Coronation Island

McMurdo Base is an active, permanent research station in Antarctica. *(Courtesy of Cicely A. Wingate)*

well stocked with scientists in all fields and of all nationalities. All the research centers worked in cooperation with one another, freely exchanging data and meeting at conferences to test their findings before an international audience.

The discoveries of the many research centers have been so extensive and varied that volumes could be written about a dozen disciplines. Leading the list of major achievements might be studies in ozone depletion, protective studies on larger marine life (whales and seals), and geological studies about the age, history, and former conditions of the continent itself. It is difficult to single out any one area of discovery when each year brings about new and unsuspected findings. In 2001, for instance, it was discovered that warm water (unfrozen) lakes exist a half mile under the South Polar ice cap. The ongoing scientific exploration is almost as exciting as the travails of Scott and Ernest Shackleton.

The torturous voyages and treks across the polar wilderness may be a thing of the past, but today's wonderful discoveries will always have the Franklins, the Scotts, the Amundsens, the Pearys, and the Byrds as their foundation. Perhaps the Canadian explorer-seaman Captain Henry Larsen, steaming through the Northeast Passage in 1944, most aptly described the present age and its relationship to the polar expeditions of earlier times: "Tribute is due to those early explorers; their sacrifices and exploits blazed most of the trail we took."

GLOSSARY

antipodes Ancient Greek name for the inhabitants of the southern continent, Antarctica. In Greek the term means "opposite feet," a reference to the fact that the ancients believed the feet of any people living on the "bottom" of the globe must have faced in the opposite direction of people's feet in the Northern Hemisphere.

archipelago A sea or smaller body of water containing many islands; also a group of such islands.

aurora borealis From the Latin for "northern dawn," the beautiful streamers of light that flash across the nighttime sky of the Arctic and subarctic. The light streams are variable in length, duration, and color (although green usually dominates). The northern lights, as the aurora borealis is commonly called, are caused by solar activity.

bay A body of water off an ocean or a sea. In size, a bay is considered to be smaller than a gulf.

Beaufort scale Devised in 1805 by British rear admiral Sir Francis Beaufort, this scale rates the speed of winds on a scale from 0 to 17. (Beaufort's original scale was based on the wind's effect on sailboats.) 0—"calm"—is less than 1 mile per hour; 6—"strong breeze"—is 25–31 miles per hour; 12 to 17—"hurricane"—is 74 miles per hour and above.

black ice A type of ice that forms, not on water, but from the freezing of mist or fog onto every exposed surface. Black ice occurs when the air is very cold; it is not white, but clear, so it appears to take on the coloration of the objects it coats.

British Admiralty The department of the British government, often called the Admiralty, that oversees naval affairs; the equivalent of the U.S. Department of the Navy.

cairn A pile of stones or ice blocks, four to seven feet high, used as storage for food, clothing, or messages, or as a grave. Most important, a cairn was used as a marker or signpost.

calving The process by which the leading edge of a glacier breaks off into the ocean and floats away as an iceberg. The term is borrowed from that used to refer to the birth of a calf.

cannibalize In the context of those explorers or others who are close to dying from starvation, to practice cannibalism, or the eating of human flesh.

cape A projection of land into surrounding water. A cape is generally broader than a peninsula and is joined to the mainland by land that is relatively close in width to its outermost portion.

channel A passage of water that connects two other bodies of water. When used to define waterways in the Arctic, a channel is almost always longer and broader than a strait.

crevasse　An opening in a glacier that might be inches or many feet wide, and several or hundreds of feet deep. Frequently crevasses are covered over with a thin layer of snow and thus presented great danger to the explorers who constantly had to cross over or around them. A well-trained lead dog (in a sled dog team) could usually sense a crevasse and warn the team driver (hopefully) in time to stop.

depot　In the context of overland exploration, a small storage installation where food and other necessities are placed so that a party can replenish itself while on a long journey.

fool's gold　A mineral (pyrite) containing iron disulfide; in its natural state it has yellowish particles that have often misled people to think it is gold.

gale　Between a strong breeze and a storm on the Beaufort scale, with winds from 32 to 63 miles per hour. Often, however, *gale* is used to mean a strong wind or generally nasty weather.

gangrene　The death and decay of bodily tissue caused by insufficient blood supply; it usually occurred after injury to or operation on a limb.

gill　Four fluid ounces in U.S. system of measurement (closer to five U.S. ounces in the British system).

glacier　Frozen rivers formed by the accumulation of snowfall under pressure into thick, deep, slow-flowing sheets of ice. Because ice is plastic, the glacier moves of its own weight until it reaches sea level. At that point, the glacier eventually breaks off and forms icebergs.

glacier tongue　A floating, narrow extension of a glacier, usually as it flows through a channel or valley; eventually the extended end of it will break away and float off as an iceberg.

gulf　An extension of an ocean or sea; smaller than a sea, but larger than a bay.

hard tack　A hard baked biscuit made of little more than flour and water; it was the standard ration on ships at sea because it did not spoil easily.

head　The outermost part of a projection of land into the surrounding water.

homeothermous　From the Greek for "same temperature," it refers to maintaining a relatively stable body temperature independent of the environment.

horst　A raised rock mass, surrounded on both sides by a fault or a break in the stratification.

hydrography　From the Greek for "water recording," the scientific study of bodies of water.

ice floe　A moderate-size piece of floating ice.

ice pack　The ice covering large areas such as the entire Arctic Ocean in winter. It is always in motion, and with warm weather and severe wave action, it will break up into pack ice.

ice shelf　A glacier (or ice sheet) that has built up at the coast, sometimes to a depth of 200 feet or more. As it extends further out into the water, it still remains attached to the coast. When its furthest edge is no longer sufficiently supported underneath, it breaks off and becomes a tabular iceberg.

inlet　A small body of water running inland from a larger body of water. It is usually quite shallow and always comes to a dead end.

krill　A group of tiny shrimplike marine animals that form the main diet of certain whales, penguins, and other creatures that feed in the ocean.

lead　Pronounced "leed," a width of open water that opens in the pack ice. A lead may vary from a few inches to hundreds of yards. Leads may open up and close quickly, without warning.

muskeg A farm tractor, modified to move through deep snow or over ice; the motor was adapted to start and function in extreme cold. The muskeg was mainly used in Antarctica.

pack ice Sheets of ice, sometimes smooth, but more often jammed together in layers and heaps, always in motion by wind and sea action.

pemmican A foodstuff prepared from meat from which all fluid has been evaporated. The dried fibers are then mixed and pounded with an equal weight of animal fat (and sometimes with dried berries or nuts). The resulting product is nourishing and lightweight and will not spoil.

peninsula A body of land surrounded by water on three sides and connected to the mainland by a narrow strip known as an isthmus.

point A small landmass that protrudes out from the shoreline into the surrounding water.

pole of inaccessibility The point in Antarctica furthest from approach by ship.

pressure ridge An irregular ice form on a frozen ocean or sea caused by sheets of ice forced together. Since there is no place for the colliding ice layers to go, they usually buckle upward.

protozoa A large group of single-celled, usually microscopic organisms.

rookery The breeding ground on land for birds or sea animals.

scurvy Disease caused by a deficiency of vitamin C; its symptoms include spongy and bleeding gums and bleeding under the skin.

sledge A vehicle with runners like a sled but drawn by work animals such as dogs or horses; it is used to transport loads across snow or rough ground.

Sno-Cat The work-horse vehicle of polar travel since the 1940s, this vehicle has an enclosed (warm) cab, and two steel treads front and back. The Sno-Cat can deal with almost any terrain, but it requires a lot of fuel.

snow beacon A trail marker, or a locator of provisions stocked for a return trip. Made of shiny and reflective material, it shines like a light in the sun and is highly visible during a snowstorm as a dark object.

snow blindness Temporary blindness caused by exposure of the unprotected eyes to the glare of sun reflecting off ice and snow. The blindness and excruciating pain lasts for several days; each attack leaves the explorer more susceptible to another. To protect themselves, the Inuit use bone or horn "glasses" with a narrow slit to see through.

snow bridge A thin covering of snow over a hidden crevasse. A snow bridge is usually unable to support a person, let alone a dog team.

sound A passage of water connecting other bodies of water. The term, as used as a place-name in the Arctic, is hardly distinguishable from a strait. Sometimes *sound* is used when a large body of water is connected to a smaller one.

strait Water that connects two other larger bodies of water. In the Arctic and the sub-arctic, straits, because they tend to be shallow, were often frozen solid the year round.

tundra The permanently frozen Arctic terrain between the frozen ice cap to the north and the forest to the south; it supports only low-growing vegetation.

ventifact A large stone mass, shaped into sculpturelike figures and objects by wind-blown sand. Ventifacts are found in the dry valleys of Antarctica.

Weasel A lightweight motorized vehicle with steel tracks, made to travel over ice or through heavy snow.

FURTHER INFORMATION

NONFICTION

Alexander, Bryan. *The Vanishing Arctic.* New York: Checkmark Books, 1997.

Alexander, Caroline. *The Endurance: Shackleton's Legendary Antarctic Expedition.* New York: Knopf, 1999.

Amundsen, Roald. *My Life as an Explorer.* New York: Doubleday & Page, 1927.

———. *The North West Passage.* London: A. Constable, 1908.

———. *The South Pole.* London: John Murray, 1912.

Anderson, William R., with Clay Blair. *Nautilus –90° North.* Cleveland, Ohio: World Publishing, 1959.

Baird, Patrick. *The Polar World.* New York: John Wiley, 1964.

Bancroft, Ann, and Liv Arnesen, with Cheryl Dahle. *No Horizon Is So Far: Two Women and Their Extraordinary Journey across Antarctica.* New York: Da Capo Press, 2003.

Barrow, John. *A Chronological History of Voyages into Arctic Regions.* London: John Murray, 1818.

Beattie, Oliver, and John Geiger. *Frozen in Time: The Fate of the Franklin Expedition.* London: Bloomsbury, 1987.

Berton, Pierre. *The Arctic Grail: The Quest for the North West Passage and the North Pole, 1818–1909.* New York: Viking, 1988.

Bertram, Colin. *Arctic and Antarctic.* Cambridge, U.K.: W. Heffer & Sons, 1958.

Byrd, Richard E. *Alone.* New York: Putnam, 1938.

Cameron, Ian. *Antarctica: The Last Continent.* London: Cassell & Co., 1974.

Cherry-Garrard, Apsley. *The Worst Journey in the World: Antarctica 1910–1913.* London: Chatto & Windus, 1937.

Cook, Frederick A. *To the Top of the Continent.* New York: Doubleday, Page & Co., 1908.

Cookman, Scott. *Ice Blink: The Tragic Fate of Sir John Franklin's Lost Polar Expedition.* New York: John Wiley, 2000.

Delgado, James P. *Across the Top of the World: The Quest for the Northwest Passage.* Vancouver, Canada: Douglas & McIntyre, 1999.

DeLong, Edward, ed. *The Voyage of the Jeanette: The Ship and Ice Journals of George W. DeLong.* New York: Houghton, Mifflin, 1884.

Fleming, Fergus. *Ninety Degrees North.* New York: Grove Press, 2001.

Fogg, G. E., and David Smith. *The Explorations of Antarctica.* London: Cassells & Co., 1990.

Franklin, John. *Narrative of a Journey to the Shores of the Polar Sea.* London: John Murray, 1823.

Gorman, James. *The Total Penguin.* Eaglewood Cliffs, N.J.: Prentice Hall Press, 1990.

Gurney, Alan. *Below the Convergence: Voyages Toward Antarctica, 1699–1839.* New York: Norton, 1997.

———. *The Race to the White Continent.* New York: Norton, 2000.

Hayes, Isaac. *The Open Polar Sea.* New York: Hurd & Houghton, 1867.

Henson, Matthew. *A Negro Explorer at the North Pole*. 1912. Reprint, New York: Arno Press, 1969.

Herbert, Wally. *Across the Top of the World: The Last Great Journey on Earth*. New York: G. P. Putnam's & Sons, 1971.

Holland, Clive, ed. *Arctic Exploration and Development, c. 500 B.C. to 1915: An Encyclopedia*. New York: Garland, 1994.

———. *Farthest North*. London: Robinson Publishing, 1990.

Kane, Elisha C. *The U.S. Grinnel Expedition in Search of Sir John Franklin*. New York: Harper, 1854.

Kirwan, L. P. *A History of Polar Exploration*. New York: W. W. Norton & Co., 1959.

Land, Barbara. *The New Explorers: Women in Antarctica*. New York: Dodd & Mead, 1981.

Landis, Marilyn. *Antarctica*. Chicago: Chicago Review Press, 2001.

Lehane, Brendan, and the Editors of Time-Life Books. *The Northwest Passage*. Alexandria, Va.: Time-Life Books, 1981.

Lopez, Barry. *Arctic Dreams: Imagination and Dreams in a Northern Landscape*. New York: Charles Scribner's Sons, 1986.

Magnusson, Magnus, ed. *The Icelandic Sagas*. London: Folio Society, 1999.

Mawson, Douglas. *The Home of the Blizzard*. London: Heinemann, 1915.

Maxton-Graham, John. *Safe Return Doubtful: The Heroic Age of Polar Exploration*. New York: Scribner's, 1988.

McClintock, Leopold. *The Voyage of the Fox in the Arctic Seas*. London: John Murray, 1859.

McClure, Robert. *The Discovery of the North-West Passage*. Edmonton, Canada: M. G. Hurtig, 1969.

Mills, William James. *Exploring Polar Frontiers: A Historical Encyclopedia*. 2 vols. Santa Barbara, Calif.: ABC-Clio, 2003.

Moss, Sanford, and Lucia deLeiris. *Natural History of the Antarctic Peninsula*. New York: Columbia University Press, 1988.

Mountfield, David. *A History of Polar Exploration*. New York: Dial Press, 1974.

Nansen, Fridtjof. *Farthest North*. New York, London: Harper & Brothers, 1898.

———. *In Northern Mists: Arctic Exploration in Early Times*, vols. I and II. New York: Frederick A. Stokes, 1911.

Naveen, Ron, Colin Monteath, Tui de Roy, and Mark Jones. *Wild Ice*. Washington, D.C.: Smithsonian Institution Press, 1991.

Neatby, L. H. *Discovery in Russian and Siberian Waters*. Athens: Ohio University Press, 1973.

Nordenskiöld, Adolf Erik. *The Voyage of the Vega Around Asia and Europe*, vols. I and II. London: Macmillan, 1881.

Officer, Charles, and Jake Page. *A Fabulous Kingdom*. New York: Oxford Press, 2001.

Parry, William Edward. *Journal of a Voyage for the Discovery of a North-West Passage from the Atlantic to the Pacific*. London: John Murray, 1821.

Peary, Robert. *Nearest the Pole*. London: Hutchinson & Co., 1907.

———. *The North Pole*. New York: Frederick A. Stokes, 1910.

Plaisted, Ralph. "How I Reached the North Pole on a Snowmobile." *Popular Science* 193 (September 1968), pp. 55–59.

Rae, John. *Expedition to the Shores of the Arctic Sea, 1846–7*. London: T & W Boone, 1850.

Rosove, Michael H., ed. *Let Heroes Speak: Antarctic Explorers, 1772–1922*. New York: Berkley Books, 2000.

Ross, James Clark. *A Voyage of Discovery and Research in the Southern and Antarctic Regions, During the Years 1839–43*. London: Latimer, Trend & Co., 1969.

Scoresby, William. *An Account of the Arctic Regions*. 1820. Reprint, New York: A. M. Kelley, 1969.

Scott, Robert F. *The Voyage of Discovery*, vols. I and II. New York: Charles Scribner's Sons, 1907.

Shackleton, Ernest. *Heart of the Antarctic*. Philadelphia: J. B. Lippincott, 1909.

Solomon, Susan. *The Coldest March: Scott's Fatal Antarctic Expedition*. New Haven, Conn.: Yale University Press, 2001.

Spufford, Francis. *I May Be Some Time: Ice and the English Imagination*. London: Faber & Faber, 1996.

Stefansson, Vilhjalmur. *The Friendly Arctic.* New York: Macmillan, 1921.

———. *The Three Voyages of Martin Frobisher in Search of a Passage to Cathay and India by the North-West, A.D. 1576–8.* London: Argonaut Press, 1938.

Steger, Will. *North to the Pole.* New York: Times Books, 1987.

Steward, John. *Antarctica: An Encyclopedia.* Jefferson, N.C.: McFarland & Co., 1990.

Swaney, Deanna. *The Arctic.* Melbourne, Australia: Lonely Planet Publications, 1999.

Tingey, Robert J.,ed. *The Geology of Antarctica.* New York: Oxford Press, 1991.

Vaughan, Richard. *The Arctic: A History.* Phoenix Mill, U.K.: Sutton Publishing, 1994.

Wilkins, Hubert. *Flying the Arctic.* New York: G. P. Putman & Sons, 1928.

Woodman, David C. *Unravelling the Franklin Mystery.* Montreal, Kingston, Canada: McGill-Queen's University Press, 1991.

Worsley, Frank. *Shackleton's Boat Journey.* New York: W. W. Norton & Co., 1977.

FICTION

Arthur, Elizabeth. *Antarctic Navigation: A Novel.* New York: Knopf, 1995.

Bainbridge, Beryl. *The Birthday Boys.* New York: Carroll & Graf, 1995.

Barrett, Andrea. *Voyage of the Narwhal.* New York: W. W. Norton & Co., 1998.

Brown, Cassie. *Death on the Ice.* Toronto: Doubleday, 1972.

Colombo, John Robert, ed. *Poems of the Inuit.* Ottawa: Oberon Press, 1981.

Cooper, James Fenimore. *The Sea Lions.* Boston: Houghton, Mifflin, 1884.

Edric, Robert. *The Broken Lands: A Novel of Arctic Disaster.* New York: Thomas Dunne Books, 2002.

Houston, James M. *The Ice Master: A Novel of the Arctic.* Toronto: McClelland & Stewart, 1999.

Kavaler, Lucy. *Heroes and Lovers: An Antarctic Obsession.* New York: Universe, 2000.

Lundy, Derek. *The Way of a Ship.* Toronto: Alfred A. Knopf, 2002.

Michener, James. *Journey.* New York: Random House, 1989.

Mowat, Farley. *The Curse of the Viking Grave.* Toronto: McClelland & Stewart, 1973.

———. *Lost in the Barrens.* New York: Bantam Books, 1985.

Norman, Howard, ed. *Northern Tales: Traditional Stories of Eskimo and Indian Peoples.* New York: Pantheon Books, 1990.

Oman, Inupiaq Lela Kiana. *The Epic of Qayaq: The Longest Story Ever Told by My People.* Ottawa: Carlton University Press, 1995.

Ransmayr, Christoph. *The Terrors of Ice and Darkness.* New York: Grover Weidenfield, 1991.

Sundman, Per Olaf. *The Flight of the Eagle: A Documentary Novel.* New York: Pantheon, 1970.

Verne, Jules. *An Antarctic Mystery.* 1897. Reprint, Ridge, N.J.: Gregg Press, 1975.

Vollmann, William. *The Ice Shirt.* New York: Viking, 1993.

VHS/DVD

Antarctica: An Adventure of a Different Nature (1996). Image Entertainment, 2000. VHS/DVD.

Arctic and Antarctica (1996). DK Eyewitness Video, 1996. VHS.

The Call of the Wild (1997). Hallmark Home Entertainment, 1998. VHS.

Douglas Mawson: The Survivor (1982). Australian Broadcasting Corp. 2003. DVD.

The Endurance: Shackleton's Legendary Antarctic Expedition (2000). HighBridge Company, 2000. VHS/DVD.

Glory and Honor (1998). Turner Home Video, 1999. VHS.

Great Adventures: Robert Falcon Scott—the Race to the Pole (1999). Kultur Video, 1999. VHS.

Last Place on Earth (1986). Bfs Entertainment & Multimedia, 2001. DVD.

Nanook of the North (1922). Kino Video, 1998. VHS/DVD.

Never Cry Wolf (1983). Anchor Bay Entertainment, 2003. VHS/DVD.

90 Degrees South: With Scott to the Antarctica (1999). Image Entertainment, 1999. DVD.

Northwest Passage (1999). Superior Productions, 1999. VHS.

Shackleton—the Greatest Survival Story of All Time (2001). A&E Home Video, 2002. VHS/DVD.

Shackleton's Antarctic Adventure (2001). Image Entertainment, 2002. DVD.

South—Ernest Shackleton and the Endurance Expedition (1999). Image Entertainment, 2000. VHS/DVD.

The Thing (1982). Universal Studios, 2002. DVD.

The White Dawn (1974). Paramount, 1986. VHS.

White Fang (1991). Disney Studios, 2002. VHS.

With Byrd at the South Pole (1999). Image Entertainment, 2000. VHS/DVD.

WEB SITES

Antarctic

GENERAL

Center for Astrophysical Research in Antarctica. "The South Pole Adventure Web Page." Available online. URL: http://astro.uchicago.edu/cara/southpole.edu. Updated on February 6, 2002.

EXPLORATION

The Antarctic Circle. Available online. URL: http://www.antarctic-circle.org. Updated on January 15, 2004.

Exploratorium: Origins—Looking Into Our Search for Beginnings. "Antarctica: Scientific Journeys from McMurdo to the Pole." Available online. URL: http://www.exploratorium.edu/origins/antarctica. Downloaded on January 4, 2004.

Arctic

GENERAL

Industry Canada. "Canadian Arctic Profiles." Available online. URL: http://collections.ic.gc.ca/arctic/english.htm. Downloaded on January 4, 2004.

National Oceanic and Atmospheric Administration. "Arctic Theme Page." Available online. URL: http://www.arctic.noaa.gov/exploration.html. Downloaded on January 4, 2004.

EXPLORATION BIBLIOGRAPHY

National Library of Canada. "Arctic Exploration and the Search for the Northwest Passage in the First Half of the Nineteenth Century." Available online. URL: http://www.nlcbnc.ca/2/21/indexe.html. Updated March 4, 2001.

Explorers

The Frederick A. Cook Society. Available online. URL: http://www.cookpolar.org. Updated in December 2002.

Matthew A. Henson. Available online. URL: http://www.matthewhenson.com. Downloaded on January 4, 2004.

Robert E. Peary, USN. Available online. URL: http://robertepeary.com. Downloaded on January 4, 2004.

Sir Ernest Henry Shackleton. Available online. URL: http://indigo.ie/~jshack. Downloaded on January 4, 2002.

South-Pole.com. "Robert Falcon Scott." Available online. URL: http://www.south-pole.com/p0000089.htm. Downloaded on January 15, 2004.

STEM~Net. "Elementary Themes: European Explorers." Available online. URL: http://www.stemnet.nf.ca/CITE/explorer.htm. Updated in May 2002.

INDEX

Page numbers in *italics* indicate a photograph. Page numbers followed by *m* indicate maps. Page numbers followed by *g* indicate glossary entries. Page numbers in **boldface** indicate box features.